LANGUAGE AND STRUCTURE
IN TENNYSON'S POETRY

THE LANGUAGE LIBRARY

EDITED BY ERIC PARTRIDGE AND SIMEON POTTER

The Best English	*G. H. Vallins*
Better English	*G. H. Vallins*
Caxton and His World	*N. F. Blake*
Chamber of Horrors	*'Vigilans'*
Changing English	*Simeon Potter*
Dictionaries: British and American (revised)	*J. R. Hulbert*
A Dictionary of Sailor's Slang	*Wilfred Granville*
Early English	*John W. Clark*
English Biblical Translation	*A. C. Partridge*
English Dialects	*G. L. Brook*
The English Language	*Ernest Weekley*
Etymology	*A. S. C. Ross*
Good English: How to Write It	*G. H. Vallins*
A Grammar of Style	*A. E. Darbyshire*
A History of the English Language	*G. L. Brook*
An Introduction to the Scandinavian Languages	*M. O'C Walshe*
Jane Austen's English	*K. C. Phillipps*
Joysprick: An Introduction to the Language of James Joyce	*Anthony Burgess*
Language and Structure in Tennyson's Poetry	*F. E. L. Priestley*
The Language of the Book of Common Prayer	*Stella Brook*
The Language of Dickens	*G. L. Brook*
The Language of Renaissance Poetry	*A. C. Partridge*
The Language of Science	*T. H. Savory*
Modern Linguistics	*Simeon Potter*
The Pattern of English	*G. H. Vallins*
The Pitcairnese Language	*A. S. C. Ross*
Sense and Sense Development	*R. A. Waldron*
Spelling	*G. H. Vallins*
Swift's Polite Conversations	*Eric Partridge*
Tudor to Augustan English	*A. C. Partridge*
The Words we Use	*J. A. Sheard*

F. E. L. Priestley

𝕊𝕊𝕊𝕊𝕊𝕊𝕊𝕊𝕊𝕊𝕊𝕊𝕊𝕊𝕊𝕊𝕊𝕊𝕊𝕊𝕊𝕊𝕊𝕊𝕊𝕊

LANGUAGE AND STRUCTURE IN TENNYSON'S POETRY

𝕊𝕊𝕊𝕊𝕊𝕊𝕊𝕊𝕊𝕊𝕊𝕊𝕊𝕊𝕊𝕊𝕊𝕊𝕊𝕊𝕊𝕊𝕊𝕊𝕊𝕊

ANDRE DEUTSCH

First published 1973 by
André Deutsch Limited
105 Great Russell Street, London WC1

Copyright © 1973 by F. E. L. Priestley
All rights reserved

Printed in Great Britain by
William Clowes & Sons, Limited
London, Beccles and Colchester

ISBN 0 233 96390 9

Contents

𓆩𓆩𓆩𓆩𓆩𓆩

Introduction

🕸🕸🕸🕸🕸

THE language of a poet is the medium of his art; it is what paint
is to the painter, or clay and stone to the sculptor. To write about
a poet's language is consequently to write about his art: to discuss
his poetry and his technique, how he uses words to create his poetic
structures, what he makes words do in achieving his artistic ends.
It is impossible to isolate any use he makes of language from the
structure he uses it in, without ignoring the essential fact of his
artistry, just as it is impossible to discuss a painter's colours and
brushwork in isolation from the actual paintings they are employed
in. The choice and arrangement of words into what we call styles,
or into metrical patterns, or into tonal harmonies, are all related in
the poet's creative activity to his aim in a particular work of art,
a poem. Moreover, it is characteristic of great artists that their
art is not static; they do not repeat even their successes. They
experiment constantly, learning by failure and by success, gaining
more and more control over their medium, trying constantly new
forms, exploring steadily the resources of the medium and the
vitality of untried structures.

It is this theme of experiment and exploration in Tennyson's
verbal art that this book is concerned with. As the reader will
recognize, no single volume can trace such a complex subject as
the development of a major poet's art, of his skill in handling his
medium, in any but a selective manner. Volumes have indeed been
written simply on his use of language in natural description, and
on the poetic structure of single major poems, like *Maud*, *In
Memoriam*, and *Idylls of the King*. Other volumes could easily be
written on his metrics, or on his use of tonal patterns. What this
work tries to do is to trace some of the major directions of
Tennyson's development and experimentation, using some very
detailed analysis of individual poems, some more general analysis

of structure of larger poems, sometimes with the intention of illustrating what seem fruitful modes of analysis for seeing what the poet is actually doing, sometimes to correct what seem to be common critical misapprehensions. It has been impossible, within the limits of space, to discuss every aspect of every poem, or to discuss every poem the reader and I would have liked to cover: the aim has been to deal with as many of the important poems as possible, while drawing attention to as many aspects of the poet's art as possible. I shall be satisfied if I have succeeded, within these limits, in giving the reader any fresh insight into Tennyson's artistry.

The arrangement of the chapters follows what appear to me the main phases of his development. To some extent these phases occur chronologically, but not narrowly so. The very young poet is naturally preoccupied with learning the first stages of mastery of his medium, and is also filled with a sense of excitement as he discovers the immense resources of language, endowed too with a large confidence in the potentialities of the medium, if only he can gain complete control of it. His experiments are consequently centred on exploring various styles, metres, stanza forms, tonal patterns, and on conveying vividly his own rich and exciting experience. The focus for his composition tends to be the stanza, or the verse paragraph; his eye is inevitably more on detail than on total pattern. The second phase is that in which he sees the necessity of composing a 'shape', a complete structure, in which detail is no longer delighted in for its own sake, but is subordinated to the purpose of the whole. In the next phase he concentrates on thoughts about various structures seen, not as metrical patterns, but as genres or kinds of poem. This develops into experimentation with genre, and the inventing of new ones. Finally, particularly for the Romantic poet, a phase of a different order from these, growing out of less purely aesthetic concerns, modifies his whole attitude towards his medium. This phase overlaps chronologically those that are primarily aesthetic and artistic; it is governed by his maturing as a person. He enters upon a range of experience not readily translatable into words, even defying translation, and comes to realize the limitations of language. This realization has also its aesthetic and artistic implications, since it presents new problems in the use of the medium. What language cannot do directly it must be made to do indirectly. Tennyson's attempts to achieve this end are the subject of the last two chapters, where it will again be apparent that the treatment is illustrative and suggestive rather than exhaustive.

The text used throughout is that edited by Christopher Ricks (Longmans *Annotated English Poets* series). The Royal Society of Canada has kindly permitted me to use material on *The Princess* first published in its *Transactions* (Fourth series, vol. 1, 1963, pp. 295–304).

Toronto, 1971   F. E. L. PRIESTLEY

CHAPTER I

Youthful Experiments

🜲🜲🜲🜲🜲🜲

ONE of the most charming and revealing of literary anecdotes is that of the young Keats, during his reading of Chapman's Homer, crying out 'sea-shouldering whales' as he moved about the room, his own shoulders hunched forward and thrusting. It captures for all time the excitement and joyous relish roused in the young poet by the power of a phrase. Keats's familiar sonnet, *On first looking into Chapman's Homer*, is a verbal expansion of the same experience, but its meaning is illuminated by the anecdote. The 'realms of gold' are realms not only of golden themes, of new romantic visions, of 'magic casements' opening on sights of strange seas, but golden realms of language, of rich and priceless phrases. And the sense of eager discovery, of seeing, like 'stout Cortez,' a whole new world spread before him, is at once that of discovering a new world of poetic ideas, and that of having found a new world of language. It is this sense of ecstatic wonder and delight at the infinite riches of language, of new realms to be discovered in it, that gives to Keats's early poetry so strong an impression of joy and vitality. And it is this same kind of delight and sense of discovery that we find in the early poetry of Tennyson. The reviewers of his first published volumes recognized this kinship when they attacked Tennyson as another member of Keats's 'Cockney School'; their instinct was right, even if their analysis of the characteristics of the School was biased and limited.

It is probable that all young poets start with this gleeful discovery of the rich resources and flexibility of their medium; certainly those do who are to become the great virtuosi of their craft. Alexander Pope, as precocious a genius as Keats and Tennyson, but one who developed his art as he matured in what seems, superficially at least, a poetic milieu and tradition less favourable to verbal exuberance and experiment, writes in his youth lines which, in their enjoyment of the sensuous beauty of

sound and of the evocative power of language, could with little
exaggeration be called Keatsian or Tennysonian:

> O'er gold sands let rich Pactolus flow,
> And trees weep amber on the banks of Po . . .
>
> Lo! where Maeotis sleeps, and hardly flows
> The freezing Tanaïs through a waste of snows . . .
>
> To Isles of fragrance, lily-silvered vales,
> Diffusing languor in the panting gales. . . .

Like his Romantic successors, Pope shows at an early age an
enthusiasm for language, an ear sensitive to its tones, its rhythms,
its phrasings, and a delighted awareness of its evocative powers.
Like them, too, he has from the start an immense confidence in
language as a medium, and practises and disciplines himself in its
use to get the command of it which would make it do his bidding.
Unlike them, he was not, for various reasons, faced with the
problems of technique which they faced in their maturity, of trying
to communicate the almost incommunicable. These problems, as
we shall see, modified Tennyson's view of language as a medium.
But of these problems the young poet is happily unaware.

i. TENNYSON, THE SCHOOLBOY POET

Although we must always regret not having all Tennyson's boy-
hood compositions, including the 'hundreds and hundreds of lines
in the regular Popean metre' which he wrote when he was eleven
and twelve (and which, to judge from the sample satiric 'character'
in *Sea Dreams* must have developed into a rather thorough
command of the style) we are fortunate in what we have.

The earliest extant composition, a fragment of translation of
Claudian's *Rape of Proserpine*, written, Sir Charles Tennyson
believes, between Tennyson's eleventh and fourteenth year,
provides the first evidence of his extraordinary technical precocity.
It may also suggest that his 'hundreds and hundreds of lines' in
couplets explored a wide range of Pope's styles, since the couplets
bear a distinct impression of the influence of Pope's Homer, as
well as suggestions of Dryden's Virgil and of Milton's epic style.
What is most impressive, apart from the general ease of the

writing, is the success with which he achieves complex patterns of tonality and rhythm. Lines like the following:

> And Earth, Air, Ocean, find one common peace . . .
> Dim wreaths of mist his mighty sceptre shroud . . .
> Through Hell's wide halls the echoing accents ran . . .
> His hoarse waves slumbered on his noiseless bed . . .
> Through Hell's deep shadows, and the realms of day . . .

all show a sophisticated sense of metrical and harmonic subtlety astonishing in a schoolboy. Note, for example, the similarities and differences in the third and fifth of the lines quoted. The first phrase in each exploits the length of the third syllable so that the effect is of a succession of long accented syllables – 'Through *Hell's wide halls*' '*Through Hell's deep shadows*'. The variation in the central long vowel, *i* to *e*, and in the half-rhyme of *Hell's halls* as against the feminine *shadows* shows as skilful and alert an ear as the endings of the lines, where the rush of unaccented syllables in 'the echoing accents ran' gives to a line which starts with a deliberate slowing of movement a sudden quick scamper, whereas 'the realms of day' retains the deliberation of movement, the echoic 'realms' (of light) standing in antithesis to 'Hell's', and the open prolonged syllable 'day' in antithesis both literally and tonally to the 'deep shadows'. The facility with which symbol, vowel echoes and contrasts, syllabic quantities, and metrical phrases are all fused into easily moving lines would do credit to most mature poets.

Even more impressive as a work of schoolboy genius is the long fragment of a play, *The Devil and the Lady*, written when Tennyson was fourteen. It has the advantage for the reader of revealing both the genius and the schoolboy, and above all of showing the kind of fascination with language and style, the sheer delight in words and phrases, which I have spoken of. This delight is cheerfully combined with schoolboy wit and high spirits, so that the total effect, and it is a charming one, is of a staggering combination of technical skill, learned echoes and allusions, ebullient boyish spirits, and sheer animal energy. The verse this time, instead of the rhymed couplets of the Claudian translation, is blank verse – often very loose blank verse – which allows the young poet a much freer rein with word and phrase. Something of the subtle harmonies and movements of the

Claudian lines consequently occurs spasmodically rather than regularly.

We do indeed find lines and passages of lyric quality, exploiting delicate or resonant patterns of tonality:

> Visions of happiness do float before thee,
> Gay-gilded figures and most eloquent shapes,
> Moulded by Fancy's gentle fingering
> To the appearance of reality,
> With youthful expectations and fond dreams,
> All rendered sunlike by the light of youth,
> Which glances on them, flit before thine eyes . . .

> The gray cock hath not crowed, the glow-worm still
> Leads on unpaled his strain of emerald light. . . .

> The mighty waste of moaning waters lay
> So goldenly in moonlight, whose clear lamp
> With its long line of vibratory lustre
> Trembled on their dun surface, that my Spirit
> Was buoyant with rejoicings. Each hoar wave
> With crispèd undulation arching rose,
> Thence falling in white ridge with sinuous slope
> Dashed headlong to the shore and spread along
> The sands its tender fringe of creamy spray. . . .

> Then came a band of melancholy sprites,
> White as their shrouds and motionlessly pale
> Like some young Ashwood when the argent Moon
> Looks in upon its many silver stems.
> And thrice my name was syllabled i' the air
> And thrice upon the wave, like that loud voice
> Which through the deep dark night i' the olden time
> Came sounding o'er the lone Ionian. . . .
> The cool and pearly gray of dawn hath crept
> Into the sable bosom of the night.

But such passages do not set the tone of this high-spirited performance; they serve rather to inject into a dominantly comic and often burlesque drama notes of the serious and lyrically beautiful, so that the tone at times hovers between the mocking and the serious. To suggest that this effect is deliberate might seem to imply an impossible degree of literary sophistication in a fourteen-year-old schoolboy, but it is noteworthy that this is precisely the effect so often used by the mature Tennyson.

The dominant tones are set by the plot and characters. The plot, as far as it goes (the play breaks off abruptly at Act III, sc. iii, l. 63), is of the *fabliau* type. Magus, a necromancer with a young wife, Amoret, is about to undertake a journey. Fearing for his wife's chastity during his absence, he summons up a devil whom he enjoins to guard her. The devil adopts the method of assuming the appearance of Amoret and intercepting successive admirers on their way to her. By the beginning of Act III, he has six of them assembled with him in a cottage, where he torments them and foments their discord until a knocking at the door makes them all seek cover. The knocking marks the return of Magus, who, after being reassured by the devil that Amoret is still safe asleep, dismisses him. In the last scene, which is incomplete, the devil returns to the cottage to mislead and torment the suitors further. The ending which never got written would presumably have followed the tradition of such tales in folklore by disclosing that while the devil was busy with his six suitors Amoret was busy with a more wily seventh.

The characters, as is customary in the genre, are stock figures. Magus and Amoret are of the type of Chaucer's January and May, with the added elements, in the case of Magus, of the necromancer. The devil is the devil of comic folklore, tailed and smelling of the pit. The six suitors are characterized by their occupations: a lawyer, an apothecary, a sailor, an astronomer-geometrician, a monk, and a soldier, all stock targets in comedy and in folklore. The young Tennyson follows tradition in developing the occupational types of the suitors: their speech is filled with the jargon of their calling, and larded with similes and metaphors drawn exclusively from their special knowledge. The wit of the author, in this mode of writing, must appear in the ingenuity of the images and comparisons wherewith he can furnish his characters, and in a kind of outrageous exuberance in the use of trade-jargon. Tennyson is particularly clever in his inventions for Pharmaceutus, the apothecary, for Stephanio, the sailor, and for Angulo, the astronomer-geometrician. 'Did you speak verity, my oil of Roses?' 'Wilt unveil then, My liniment of Linseed, my Electuary, My syrup of Poppies, eh? my flower of sulphur?' Where ingenuity falters, sheer exuberance lends energy, as in the apothecary's objurgations: 'Bole! Borax! Blister! Balsam! Bark! ... Galls! garlic! ginger! guiacum!' where explosive tonalities and rhythms combine with unpleasant associations in a purely incantatory use of language. Stephanio's speech is so brilliantly overstuffed with nautical jargon and similes as to make him the ultimate in stage sailors, and here again exuberance in the use of language is more dominant than wit. Angulo perhaps combines both in most equal measure, particularly in his exchanges with the devil. We shall have occasion below to examine some of his lines further.

Benedict, the monk, and Campano, the soldier, are given the most conventional and perfunctory treatment, and it is clear that they failed to rouse the young poet's excited interest to the same degree as the others. They do, however, join in some of the entertaining *ensembles*, where Tennyson exploits the comedy of quick interchanges among the suitors, each using his own jargon, as in Act II, sc. vi, where the comic effects play rapidly on each other – again a surprisingly sophisticated effect for so young a dramatist.

Magus and the devil are rather more complicated in their development. Each of them is given a number of long speeches: four entire short scenes (I. ii, II. i, II. iii and II. vii) consist solely of soliloquies by the devil; I. iii is given entirely to a soliloquy by Magus, who has two other soliloquies in I. i and III. ii. The devil has a long speech in I. v, and Magus another in III. ii. The devil's first soliloquy is in a low style, continuing the first impression made at his entrance, where his facetious heroics lead Magus to describe him as 'the most impertinent Devil That ever smelt bitumen!' At this point he is being developed simply as a low comic character:

> O STYX AND ACHERON!
> What deprecations, amulets and charms,
> What exorcisms, crossings and bead countings,
> What Ave-Maries will be played against me!
> I value not your amulets and charms
> The twentieth part of half a rotten murphy
> Or a split pea, albeit I do confess me
> I'm apt to turn tail on an Ave-Mary,
> And quail a little at a Pater-Noster,
> Except when it's said backwards.

The same spirit of flippancy is continued, although with a more refined style, in I. v, as he speaks to Amoret:

> Now, now, my dainty one, my delicate ward,
> My pretty piece of frail mortality,
> Where think you is the rendezvous of Saints,
> Where their celestial club-room, that you make
> A fretwork argent of your snowy fingers,
> And cast your jetty pupils up on high
> Until the blank, unanimated white
> Usurps the field of vision?

The delicately mannered verse, especially the 'fretwork argent' and the mocking elaboration of the rolled-up eyes, suggests at once by its style a much more subtle devil than the pantomime figure of the opening. As the speech continues, we recognize the sort of Satanic inversion of values belonging to a much more serious tradition of diabolism:

> There is a Heaven beneath this Earth as fair
> As that which roofs it here.
> Dost think that Heaven is local, and not rather
> The omnipresence of the glorified
> And liberated Spirit – the expansion
> Of man's depressed and fettered faculties
> Into omniscience?

The argument is essentially that of Milton's Satan tempting Eve, with distorted echoes of the 'Paradise within thee happier far' and 'Where'er I am is Hell, myself am Hell!'. Tennyson has very rapidly become dissatisfied with a pantomime devil, and is developing something much more complicated. He does this not simply by the content of the speeches, but equally by control of language and style. In the same scene he gives the devil a speech of rebuke to Amoret in which the style has power and dignity:

> Faith and troth, Madam, if my fates had bid me
> To tread the thorny path of life with thee . . .
> Would I become a target of your taunts? . . .
> Would I be hurried like the dust of the earth
> With every gale of passion to and fro,
> Or be the plaything of your haughtiness
> To gibe and sneer at?

We are consequently not entirely surprised when Act II opens with a soliloquy by the devil full of philosophical musings on man, the nature of the physical world, and the ground of all

Being. But his soliloquy starts with a description of the approach of dawn so elaborately mannered as to suggest parody; a serious high style is then used for the philosophical musings. The description and the rest of the soliloquy are separated by an indicated pause, which suggests the possibility that Tennyson intends the description to be parody, his facetious devil in his polished and literate form amusing himself with a dash of Euphuism, then his more serious devil, after a pause, seriously facing the mysteries of man and the universe. In the last speech of Act I, the devil shows this same movement from facetious to serious, mockingly observing to himself, 'I am in troth a moralizing devil'. His last soliloquy (II. vii) starts with a powerful attack on the corruptness of man, and then drops quickly to a low style, ending with low prose as he prepares to join the suitors. It is of course possible that Tennyson at fourteen years of age is simply enjoying writing dialogue for a devil whose character he has not really defined to himself, and that he moves thoughtlessly from an impudent, mischievous, puck-like devil to a sententious devil possessed by some of the intellectual power and even dignity of Milton's Satan. It is also possible, however, given the extraordinary precocity shown in the play, that the young poet knows what he is doing, and is making dramatic effect out of the turns of the devil's mind, and out of the contrasts between his active *persona* and his reflective one. One wonders, for example, how many ironic implications were in Tennyson's boyish mind when in III, iii he had the devil rouse the suitors with an echo of his grandsire's call to his vanquished legions – 'Awake, arise, or be for ever fallen.'

What is of importance to this study, of course, is not to discover inconsistencies or complexities in a schoolboy's characterisation, but to recognise rather how his command of varieties of style and diction serves him in characterization. It is the control of style in the play that concerns us here; we are examining an unfinished experiment, watching the process of the young poet's own discovery of the effects to be produced by language. There are naturally, in such an attempt to probe the poet's mind in its intentions and procedures, many imponderables, many questions to which we cannot hope to find any sure answer, but I think the questions are worth asking.

One of these concerns the philosophical passages put so often into the mouths of Magus and of the devil. Many of these are not obviously humorous, although they could be for the most part written with schoolboy tongue in cheek. The subjects and the reflections on them are often trite and commonplace; is the poet aware of this and using it? Magus is clearly meant at least partly to be seen as pompous and self-important, and may deliberately be given rotund expression of the clichés of thought. The loose improvisations often given to Magus, like the one on procrastination (I.i) and the one on anxiety (I. iii) seem designed not to be taken seriously. But in all these passages the style is not as a rule overtly burlesque, but a very competent expression of well-worn ideas:

> Distrust increases with increase of years,
> She is the firstborn of Experience
> And ye may know her by her stealthy shuffle
> And the keen gray twinkle of her deep-sunk eye,
> And the rejectings of her anxious front
> To gaze at her own shadow . . .

>   The broidered side
> Of Life's fair tapestry, with its woven groups
> Of gloomy imagery, and the inwrought splendour
> Of flower and fruitage, showeth fair to the eyes
> Of inexperienced immaturity,
> But unto those whose rarity of locks
> The hand of Time hath salted, she exhibits
> The dark reverse of it,
> The intertwinings and rough wanderings
> Of random threads and wayward colourings –
> A mêlée and confusion of all hues,
> Disorder of a system which seemed Order.

The dominant impression made by a passage like this is of a young poet concentrating on the fresh expression of a commonplace idea – with a fair degree of success. And this, I think, must be the dominant impression of the play generally: due credit being given to such elements as plot-handling and characterization, it is still above all an exercise in and an exploration of varieties of style. It is certainly this which gives it its enormous gusto. The defence of caning, of the *argumentum baculinum*, put appropriately, from the schoolboy's point of view, into the mouth of the devil, is a neat and charming exercise in the ironic style:

'Tis a most delicate physic, suited to
All ages from the schoolboy to the wife.
It quickens business, makes the lazy blood,
Which heretofore was stagnant, circulate,
'Tis the primeval origin of virtue.
Moulding the mind to good, it checks the freaks
Of growing vice i' the heart; corrects the hardness
Of our ferocious natures like the iron
Which when most beaten is most ductile; thus
Men's natures are all malleable . . .

Passage after passage shows a real virtuosity in vituperation and invective, a style very dear to the heart of a schoolboy. Thus Amoret's farewell to her departed husband:

>   Go thy ways!
> Thou yellowest leaf on Autumn's withered tree!
> Thou sickliest ear of all the sheaf! Thou clod!
> Thou fireless mixture of Earth's coldest clay!
> Thou crazy dotard, crusted o'er with age
> As thick as ice upon a standing pool!
> Thou shrunken, sapless, wizen Grasshopper,
> Consuming the green promise of my youth!

This is by any standards a brilliant passage, with its movement from the withered tree of Autumn to the green promise, from the diseased sickliest ear to the consuming grasshopper, and with the neat connections from clod to coldest clay to crusted ice, and with its superb tonalities of velars and sibilants. The devil's description of Pharmaceutus is of a more conventional sort, but still written with great energy, especially in the use of hyphened terms:

> A mad, drug-dealing, vile apothecary,
> A thing of gallipots and boluses,
> Lean, lanthorn-jawed, splay-handed, pasty-faced,
> Hard-favoured and loose-jointed, ill-proportioned,
> Whose lips do roll on castors, and whose love
> Is nauseous as his physic.

Some of the liveliest scenes, in which the young Tennyson obviously delighted, consist mainly of those exchanges of imaginative insult known in medieval literature as *flytings*. The schoolboy is naturally more interested in the phrasing of an insult than of a compliment, and the one demands as much command of the resources of the language, as lively a fancy, and perhaps as good an ear for tonalities and rhythms, as the other; the first demands more vigour, the second more delicacy.

What is much less expected in a schoolboy than a talent for insult is the kind of wit dependent on a wide range of ideas, and this kind we meet with very often in *The Devil and the Lady*. The definition of wit is spoken by the devil at the beginning of Act III, when he invites Antonio to drink a little wine to 'kindle the combination of images From whose collision leaps the brilliant spark Of Heaven-born wit.' Angulo and the devil have several neat exchanges in which Angulo corrects the devil's geometry, the devil having carelessly spoken of himself as the centre of a circle, in one example, and in another used the word *point* in the sentence: 'Let me have no divisions on the point', whereupon Angulo starts an exchange by noting that a point has neither parts nor magnitude. Elsewhere we find an extended comparison of a lover to a thermometer at boiling point (80 by Réaumur's scale, and more than twice as much by Fahrenheit), and the neat comparison of wishes to a telescope, since though they 'bring far things awhile beneath the view, They cannot 'minish the long interval And space between the object and the wish.' These are of the sort of wit known as *metaphysical*; Tennyson's examples are notably successful in both the ingenuity of the comparison and the neatness of the phrasing.

It is not only in imagery that his unusual range of knowledge and intelligence appears. The devil's long soliloquy at the beginning of Act II brings in reflections hardly expected in a boy of fourteen. One might perhaps not be surprised by musings on 'the ample spheres of never-ending space' and the plurality of worlds, but it is surely unexpected to find the physical theory of Boscovich (or Priestley's modification), that solid-seeming matter may be only 'physical points Endowed with some repulsive potency'; or the paradox of infinite or finite divisibility of matter (a paradox the older Tennyson was to return to many times in later poems); or the vulgar view of Berkeley's philosophy, a doubt whether external things 'exist when none are by to view' them, that their Being may 'alone be in the mind and the intelligence of the created' (one cannot know whether it is the boy author or the devil who overlooks Berkeley's true doctrine, that they exist, not simply in the mind of the *created*, but in that of the *Creator*.) It takes a rare schoolboy even to misunderstand Berkeley.

This major fragment, then, reveals a child prodigy; a schoolboy with a wide range of reading, filling his lines with echoes and allusions, a boy with an interest in scientific and philosophical ideas, and a young poet with a great deal of technical competence and a good degree of mastery of a wide range of language. It is this last which makes, if not the most important, the most enduring impression on the reader. Apart from the neatness of the imagery, and the delight in phrases: – 'thou fulsome scrag', 'thou petticoated solecism', 'as brisk as bottled beer', 'like a bruised tinkettle', 'that demi-circle of entrails' – one notes the command over long rhetorical passages and long sustained images. Compare, for example, the rhetorical rhythms of the devil's speech to Amoret quoted in part above (p. 16) and his later one to her in the same scene:

> Begone!
> Get thee to bed – yet stay – but one word more –
> Let there be no somnambulations,
> No colloquy of soft-tongued whisperings
> Like the low hum of the delighted bee
> I' the calyx of a lily – no kerchief-waving!
> No footfalls i' the still night! Lie quietly,
> Without the movement of one naughty muscle,
> Still as a kernel in its stone, and lifeless . . .

The first passage, with its parallel rhetorical questions, 'Would I . . . ?' with its rising tone, the questions expanding from single lines to four-line periods, the whole driven along powerfully by explosive alliterations and heavy accents, suggests a mounting fury. The passage above, with its breaks and hesitations, its short, lightly accented flows, its soft tonalities, creates a sense of the softly sinister, the kind of devil's voice that insinuates, and threatens quietly, expecting its power to be known. Passages of this sort, showing an ability to build a structure of sustained rhetorical shape, and to give to each structure its own kind of movement, pace, and tonality, mark an extraordinary kind of artistic maturity.

ii. ADOLESCENCE, 1823–30

To read the rest of the poems written by Tennyson before he was twenty is to suffer some sense of disappointment. The verses published in *Poems by Two Brothers* (written mostly by Alfred and Charles, but including some by Frederick), and those written between 1823 and 1827 but not published, convey little or none of the energy and zest of *The Devil and the Lady*. Their subjects and styles are varied, and for the most part they are competently written, but they suggest almost wholly the work of a competent minor poet capturing the manner of other poets without creating a manner of his own or infusing his own vigour into the styles he is imitating. To some extent this is an effect of the main models chosen, Byron and Moore. Moore's use of easy anapaests and of conventional diction makes him easy to imitate, and in Tennyson's poems of this period one misses the metrical and harmonic complexities that are so astonishingly mature in the earlier play. There are in these later poems too many lines of the following type:

> I wander in darkness and sorrow,
> > Unfriended, and cold, and alone,
> As dismally gurgles beside me
> > The bleak river's desolate moan.

> I will hang thee, my Harp, by the side of the fountain,
> > On the whispering branch of the lone-waving willow:
> Above thee shall rush the hoarse gale of the mountain,
> > Below thee shall tumble the dark breaking billow.

> The foes of the east have come down on our shore,
> > And the state and the strength of Peru are no more:
> Oh! cursed, doubly cursed, was that desolate hour,
> > When they spread o'er our land in the pride of their power!

There are also mannerisms in the style, particularly a fondness for adverbs like *shrilly, holily, thrillingly*, and once even *blurly*. The sublime, as the ode *On Sublimity* makes clear with its allusion to Burke, tends to the Gothic:

> Thy delight
> > Is in the secret wood, the blasted heath,
> The ruined fortress, and the dizzy height,
> > The grave, the ghastly charnel-house of death,
> The vaults, in cloisters, and in gloomy piles,
> Long corridors and towers and solitary aisles.

There is, consequently, much Gothic in subject matter and in treatment.

Some of the writing, by comparison with the earlier work, is extraordinarily bad. *Antony to Cleopatra* is perhaps the worst specimen:

> O, Cleopatra! fare thee well,
> We two can meet no more;
> This breaking heart alone can tell
> The love to thee I bore . . .
> Then when the shriekings of the dying
> Were heard along the wave,
> Soul of my soul! I saw thee flying;
> I followed thee, to save . . .
> Thine on the earth, and on the throne,
> And in the grave, am I;
> And, dying, still I am thine own,
> Thy bleeding Antony.

The adolescent poet has apparently suffered an attack of Romanticism, and is temporarily debilitated by the virus. He comes closest to success in this period with two rhymed odes of free verse-length, one on Time and one on the fall of Jerusalem, and with his Cambridge prize poem, *Timbuctoo*, which incorporates much of an earlier poem on Armageddon. This last is in blank verse.

Since our concern is with the development of Tennyson's mastery of his medium, rather than with passing judgement simply on his success, we cannot ignore his failures, because they too are part of his development. What is most significant in the poems of 1823 to 1827 is that the successes are not in stanzaic form, but in relatively free rhymed ode and blank verse. Tennyson has yet to gain control of stanzas. His writing is, paradoxically, at this point tightest and most closely patterned tonally and metrically when he writes in the looser form. In the stanza, he is often writing loosely to fill out the stanza. As we shall see, the failures of this period lead him to the carefully planned experiments of the next, which are exhibited in the published volume of 1830.

If the poems of 1827 failed through an excess of imitation of the wrong models, it can be said that those of 1830 failed through an excess of experiment. The experiments undoubtedly served their purpose, but Tennyson was right in judging most of the poems not worth reprinting in later volumes. Their interest now is mainly as pieces from the artist's workshop.

A major form of experimentation is in sound effects. The best-known examples are the 'girl portraits': *Claribel, Lilian, Madeline,* and *Adeline*. The term 'girl portraits' applied to these by critics is rather misleading, in that it puts more emphasis on the content of the poems than on their form, and suggests an attempt at solid characterization which is not there. The term would be acceptable if it were understood that these are impressions, rather than portraits, conceived from a point of view as close to that of the musician as of the poet. Tennyson tries to suggest this in the subtitle to *Claribel* – 'A Melody'. He takes, in other words, a type of girl character, and tries to convey its quality partly by imagery and its associations, mainly by the musical effects of tonality, tempo, and movement – *allegro, largo, andante,* and so on – so that the character is conceived in something like abstract terms of mood and association. This is an interesting mode of experiment; in technique and intention it has a degree of resemblance to the methods later used by Swinburne. It involves going contrary to the main direction of the English poetic tradition, which relies on concrete, specific detail, and precise definition. The kind of obtuse criticism it invites is illustrated by Leigh Hunt's comment on *Lilian*: 'an instance of that injudicious crowding of images which sometimes results from Mr Tennyson's desire to impose upon us the abundance of his thoughts'. Nothing in fact could be further from Tennyson's mind; the poems are not in the least concerned with the presentation of an abundance of thoughts, nor with enabling the reader to conjure up a sharp detailed image of a flesh and blood character. The poems are not in any sense dramatic, nor are they lyrical in the sense of a presentation of the poet's reflections – they are lyrical in the sense Tennyson indicates, melodies based on an impression and a mood.

That they are not entirely successful, even on their own terms, does not destroy their importance. They might seem, in the context of received opinion about the nature of Tennyson's later poetry, to be an aberration, a path he explored, abandoned, and never returned to. The Tennyson who carefully noted the colour of ash-buds, and who rendered parts of the English landscape with photographic accuracy, has indeed nothing in common with the Tennyson of these poems. But the Tennyson of popular criticism, admired by botanists, ornithologists, and lovers of landscape, although a real Tennyson, is not the only Tennyson, and even in his most minute fidelity to the concrete, the mature poet usually fuses the sense of a more abstract significance, of a pervading mood, and of a suggestive tonality. It is the technique of rendering these that he is exploring in the 'girl portraits'.

Where they fail – and not one of them entirely succeeds – it is from his not having mastered the technique. The failure is usually in the diction. In the most nearly successful, *Claribel*, the melody is beautifully phrased, the images significant, the slow, muted movement well sustained. But the rhyme scheme has led the poet into an occasional infelicity:

> Where Claribel low-lieth
> The breezes pause and die,
> Letting the rose-leaves fall:
> But the solemn oak-tree sigheth,
> Thick-leaved, ambrosial,
> With an ancient melody
> Of an inward agony
> Where Claribel low-lieth.

Here 'ambrosial' seems to introduce associations not fitting the context. And in the second stanza, 'dwelleth' and 'lispeth' are weak, the implication of 'lispeth' being particularly bad in a poem with thirteen -*eth* endings in twenty-one lines. The opening lines of *Lilian*, 'Airy, fairy Lilian, Flitting, fairy Lilian' led the critics, perhaps understandably, to recall Namby-Pamby Philips.

The writing of this period, and of the year or two up to the publication of the following volume in 1832, is marked by a fondness for archaism and for affected diction. Sometimes this is relatively successful, as in the opening lines of the song:

> The lintwhite and the throstlecock
> Have voices sweet and clear;
> All in the bloomèd May.
> They from the blosmy brere
> Call to the fleeting year,
> If that he would them hear
> And stay.
> Alas! That one so beautiful
> Should have so dull an ear.

But it can also, as in the same song, become merely mannered:

> Thy locks are all of sunny sheen
> In rings of gold yroune,
> All in the bloomèd May.
> We prithee pass not on;
> If thou dost leave the sun,
> Delight is with thee gone,
> Oh! stay.
> Thou are the fairest of thy feres,
> We prithee pass not on.

The impression made by stanzas like these is that the poet's main attention is focused on the problems presented by the complex stanza form he has chosen, and by the melodic and formal pattern it calls for, and that his choice of diction is partly dictated by rhyme, and partly by a fascination with the archaic forms.

This impression is reinforced by considering a second general direction which the poet's experiments are clearly taking at this time. In the volume of 1830, one notes the almost complete avoidance of blank verse, the medium in which the poet had attained such mastery at so early an age. The one important exception is *The Mystic*. What we find instead is a profusion of experiments in metrical forms. There are six or seven sonnets, all trying variations on the traditional forms. *Love and Sorrow* uses eighteen lines in a most unusual pattern. It starts with the familiar *abba* rhyme of the Petrarchan form, but extends the first movement to five lines by a further *b* rhyme, *abbab*. It then begins its second movement with a triplet, rhymed *ccc*, followed without stop by a further Petrarchan *effe*. Then comes the sestet, made up here of a Petrarchan quatrain, which is a single complete sentence, then a couplet in the Shakespearian manner, except that its last line is an alexandrine. The result is a most unusual and interesting variation on the sonnet form.

The next sonnet, 'Could I outwear my present state of woe', has the conventional fourteen lines, and the usual development by octet and sestet, but a most unusual rhyme scheme, which starts with an alternate *abab*, but picks the *b* rhyme for two successive Petrarchan quatrains, *bccbbeeb*, and ends with a Shakespearian couplet. The sonnet 'Though Night hath climbed her peak of highest noon' comes closer to a traditional form, the Shakespearian, but instead of the final couplet, continues the alternate rhyme of the third quatrain, and substitutes a Petrarchan for an alternate quatrain at the first, giving a rhyme scheme *abbacdcdefefef*. The sonnet 'The pallid thunderstricken sigh for gain' uses a basically Shakespearian rhyme pattern of three quatrains and a couplet, but the quatrains are Petrarchan, and the poem divides into ten lines and four, not eight and six, so that the last half of the last quatrain flows into the final couplet. This again is a very ingenious variation.

These experiments inevitably recall those of Keats, a few years earlier, and the part played by variants on the sonnet in shaping the forms of his great odes. The fact that Tennyson chose not to reprint most of these sonnets, and that his later sonnets tend to a more conventional form (though he continues to mix Petrarchan and alternate quatrains freely) should not give the impression that these experiments are failures, nor that as experiments they were fruitless. Like Keats, Tennyson is learning the effects of rhyme patterns and of syntactical structure on the form and proportions of a poem. He is studying what might be termed principles of architecture. Like Keats, he finds the limited compass of the sonnet an admirably sized model for experiment.

His experiments in form are of course by no means limited to the sonnet. He tries a great variety of stanzaic forms, being particularly interested in the effect of the refrain, or repeated phrase. In some cases, as in the song, 'A spirit haunts the year's last hours', the refrain is the most successful part of the poem, suggesting perhaps that the rest of the poem developed as an attempted expansion of the refrain. In this particular case, the diction and tonality of the refrain:

> Heavily hangs the broad sunflower
> Over its grave i' the earth so chilly;
> Heavily hangs the hollyhock,
> Heavily hangs the tiger-lily . . .

are not well matched to those of the other lines. In the song *The Owl* refrain and verse are perfectly matched. In *Recollections of the Arabian Nights* effective use is made of a refrain with changes, only the third and fifth being identical. Each refrain until the last ends with 'the golden prime of good Haroun Alraschid', which in the last becomes 'his golden prime, The good Haroun Alraschid'. The refrain thus keeps a basic form, but rings changes on it, giving not only variety but a special emphasis on the parts varied. The most effective use of the device is in one of the finest poems in the volume, *Mariana*, where the refrain becomes a dramatic element. The whole poem is most impressive in the sureness of its technique, and is one of the earliest examples of Tennyson's mastery of a stanza form throughout a poem. The refrain is used to introduce the theme; the first stanza opens with description:

> With blackest moss the flower-plots
>   Were thickly crusted, one and all:
> The rusted nails fell from the knots
>   That held the peach to the garden-wall.
> The broken sheds looked sad and strange:
>   Unlifted was the clinking latch;
> Weeded and worn the ancient thatch
>   Upon the lonely moated grange.
> She only said, 'My life is dreary,
>   He cometh not,' she said;
> She said, 'I am aweary, aweary,
>   I would that I were dead!'

The technique of this stanza is worth some examination. The form of the stanza, apparently Tennyson's own invention, is obviously related to his experiments with the sonnet form, since the rhyme scheme *ababcddc* shows the alternate quatrain followed by a Petrarchan one so common in his sonnets. But he has chosen an octosyllabic line rather than a decasyllabic or pentameter, and has carefully retarded its movement. The refrain is written in something like ballad metre, with lines of 9, 6, 10, and 6 syllables, using alternate rhyme. Something of the quality of the ballad is thus infused into the whole poem, aided by the ballad-like repetitions in the refrain. Yet the tempo established by the main stanza is totally unballadlike, as is the subject-matter. The sharply defined descriptive detail is all focused on creating a picture of desolation and decay (in later editions Tennyson replaced 'the peach on the garden-wall' by 'the pear on the gable-wall' to remove the rich associations of 'peach' and 'garden'). The purpose, and the diction used to achieve it, are remote from the purpose and diction of a ballad. One notes, for example, that although at this time Tennyson elsewhere shows a great addiction to archaisms, there is not one in the first eight lines, and only 'cometh' in the refrain. The diction is relatively simple, and very direct, yet one is aware that this is a complex and carefully wrought passage. The rhymes are by no means common sounds, yet there is no hint that they have dictated the text. The tonal effects are brilliantly complicated, internal assonances like 'moss, plots', 'crusted, rusted', 'broken, lonely, moated', and alliterations like 'nail, knots', 'sad, strange', 'weeded, worn', and the changes of vowels rung through the lines, all mark a most sophisticated ear, yet again all fall naturally into place with no sense of strained artifice.

The methods by which the poet established the slow tempo of his octosyllabics is also noteworthy. The secret lies in the distribution, not only of accents, but of quantity. Tennyson understood, perhaps better than any English poet before him, the importance of length of vowel and syllable in English verse. His remark that he thought he knew the quantity of every English word except 'scissors' is often quoted, but the implications of the remark are not always elaborated. He realized how unsatisfactory all attempts to deal with English verse as simply accentual are, especially those attempts based on trying to find accentual 'feet' corresponding to classical quantitative ones. Classical quantities of long and short are, in theory, of fixed relationship, whatever they might be to the ear in actual recitation. Any theory that supposes any fixed relationship between accented and unaccented syllable in English gives no sense whatsoever of how the verse sounds when properly read. No two accents in a line, or perhaps even in a verse paragraph, are at all equal, nor are the amounts of stress given to any two unaccented syllables; syllables supposed by the system to be accented may have a degree of stress barely distinguishable from that given to one supposed not to be accented. Moreover, quantity, though ignored by the system, cannot be ignored by the ear. A line filled with long syllables will move more slowly than one made up of short ones. Blocks of consonants, sustained consonants such as nasals, long open vowels, all retard the line. The effects of accent can be combined with those of quantity, or can be counterpointed against them. These are the technical effects to which Tennyson gave so much thought, and over which he acquired such mastery. And *Mariana* is one of the early exhibitions of this mastery. It is admirably illustrated in the tonal shift of the last refrain. Through the first six stanzas, only the first line of the refrain has varied: 'My life is dreary', 'The night is dreary', 'The day is dreary', 'My life is dreary', 'The night is dreary', 'My life is dreary' – slight dramatic modulations, but virtually no tonal change. Now, in the final stanza, the refrain shifts abruptly:

> Then, said she, 'I am very dreary,
>   He will not come,' she said;
> She wept, 'I am aweary, aweary,
>   Oh God, that I were dead!'

Accent, quantity, and consonantal tone combine in the staccato outburst.

One other poem in the 1830 volume is of special interest, even though not a great success, *The Ballad of Oriana*. At a superficial level, it invites comparison with *Mariana*; it has connections with the tradition of the ballad, it uses an unusual stanza form, and it makes use of a refrain. A brief consideration of why it is not successful, following the discussion of *Mariana*, ought to show another aspect of Tennyson's experimentation in this period of his development.

The stanza he chose for *Oriana* is an extraordinarily rigid and static one, demanding five identical rhymes, and with the name *Oriana* recurring as a refrain after the first, second, fourth and fifth lines. The lines are octosyllabic, varied occasionally by an extra syllable. In the opening stanza the form is successful, if considered in detachment from the rest of the poem: it has a fine slow movement, retarded still more after the second refrain by the extra length, the clustered accents, and the long syllables of the fifth and sixth lines:

> My heart is wasted with my woe,
>   Oriana.
> There is no rest for me below,
>   Oriana.
> When the long dun wolds are ribbed with snow,
>   Oriana,
> Alone I wander to and fro,
>   Oriana.

Movement is virtually arrested by the suspensions at each refrain, and by the persistent, unchanging open rhyme. The verses create a fine mood of melancholy, of the elegiac.

Having created his mood and tempo in the first stanza, the daring young poet then proceeds to force the static stanza form into motion, and we realize that in this poem he is not, as in *Mariana*, intending to eliminate the action of the traditional ballad form, but is trying to present a ballad narrative, full of action, even swift action, through the medium of a form essentially static. There is a precedent for this sort of technical virtuosity, of course, in Spenser's poetry. The Spenserian stanza is also an extremely static one, and the devices by which Spenser makes it move rapidly and vigorously to describe action are worth any young poet's study. But the Spenserian stanza, with its nine lines of un-interrupted flow, offers much more room for syntactical manoeuvre than the *Oriana* stanza, and its rhyme scheme also offers much more flexibility. Tennyson is very soon in difficulties.

His second stanza achieves a good degree of pace, although if one reads it with, and then without the refrain, 'Oriana', one soon recognizes the extent of the drag upon movement the refrain creates:

> Ere the light on dark was growing,
> > Oriana,
> At midnight the cock was crowing,
> > Oriana:
> Winds were blowing, waters flowing,
> We heard the steeds to battle going,
> > Oriana;
> Aloud the hollow bugle blowing,
> > Oriana.

It is interesting to note the continuing of the same basic rhyme sound here, but in a feminine form: 'blow' in the first stanza becoming 'blowing' in this. Normally the feminine rhyme would retard, but by comparison with the open vowels of the first stanza, the two syllables move more quickly. The internal rhyme, 'blowing', 'flowing', speeds the line, as does the alliteration of 'cock' and 'crowing'. There is, however, a strong sense that here, as in the first stanza, the details have been determined by the metrical and tonal demands of the form: there seems little relevance to the action in the blowing wind and flowing waters. By the fifth stanza, the technical problems become overwhelming:

> The bitter arrow went aside,
> > Oriana:
> The false, false arrow went aside,
> > Oriana:

> The damnèd arrow glanced aside,
> And pierced thy heart, my love, my bride,
>   Oriana!
> Thy heart, my life, my love, my bride,
>   Oriana!

The demands of the form are dodged here by repetition, so that two words fill the five rhymes. But the repetitions cannot, in so sophisticated a form, be the formula repetitions of the folk ballad, and they give consequently an impression of rather lame padding. The final stanza, which, after all the action, returns to the expression of mood, is again relatively successful. *The Ballad of Oriana*, then, represents an experiment which does not succeed. As we shall see, it is an experiment which in its essentials is repeated in the two versions of *The Lady of Shalott*, to emerge finally triumphant in 1842.

iii. POEMS, 1832

The volume of Tennyson's poems published in December 1832 (dated 1833) was savagely reviewed in the *Quarterly* by J. W. Croker, notorious for his attack on Keats. Although Croker's review was much more brutal than that of the 1830 volume in *Blackwood's* by 'Christopher North' (John Wilson, the 'crusty Christopher' of Tennyson's verse rejoinder) the quality of the later volume is superior to that of the earlier. The work is still largely experimental.

The experiments in sonnet form continue. Of seven sonnets in this volume, and five others written at this time but not included (printed in Ricks, 467 ff.), only two use the same rhyme scheme. Three of those not published use the traditional Petrarchan octet rhyme, and vary only in the sestet, but only one of those published keeps the *abba abba* octet, and then continues the rhyme in a sestet of *acacac*. Another published one uses after an octet of *abba cdcd* (repeating Tennyson's earlier mixture of Petrarchan and alternate quatrain), the very unusual sestet rhyme *efgfge*, enclosing an alternate quatrain within a pair of rhymes. Octets are varied into *abba baab, abba acac, abba cddc*. It is significant that none of the sonnets use the final Shakespearian couplet, an indication that the Elizabethan patterns, both Petrarchan and Shakespearian, followed by Tennyson in his earlier sonnets, have given way to later, Romantic ones – an impression reinforced by style and subject-matter. Sonnets in the 1832 volume on such political subjects as Bonaparte, the Polish insurrection, and the Russian invasion of Poland are in the Romantic tradition of Wordsworth and his generation, a tradition that looks back to Milton as much as to the Elizabethans. The most interesting of the sonnets, the personal manifesto which serves as preface to the volume, is also in the Romantic rather than the Elizabethan mode, both in matter and in style:

> Mine be the strength of spirit, full and free,
> Like some broad river rushing down alone,
> With the selfsame impulse wherewith he was thrown
> From his loud fount upon the echoing lea: –
> Which with increasing might doth forward flee
> By town, and tower, and hill, and cape, and isle,
> And in the middle of the green salt sea
> Keeps his blue waters fresh for many a mile.
> Mine be the power which ever to its sway
> Will win the wise at once, and by degrees
> May into uncongenial spirits flow;
> Even as the great gulf-stream of Florida
> Floats far away into the Northern Seas
> The lavish growths of southern Mexico.

The view of the poet and his function expressed here is the Romantic one associated with the second generation of Romantic poets, already voiced in more simply Shelleyan terms in *The Poet* (1830). Here the images chosen are more complex than in the earlier manifesto. In *The Poet*, as in Shelley's *Defense of Poetry* (published later) the poet is seer and prophet, spreading light by the 'viewless arrows of his thoughts', 'winged with flame', scattering seeds of truth until 'the world like one great garden showed', bringing the great sunrise of freedom, and with his word shaking the world. The images are confident, not only in the poet's power, but in the world's receptiveness; like the young Shelley, the young Tennyson sees man as waiting only to be shown the truth and he will rise, throw off his shackles and blindfold, and be free. Now there is recognition of 'uncongenial spirits'; the poet's power will always 'win the wise at once', but it 'may', not 'must', flow into uncongenial spirits 'by degrees', bringing them, not the necessarily transforming vision of truth, but 'the lavish growths of southern Mexico', rich warmth and life from the land of the sun, a little life to their 'Northern Seas'. No longer is there an explicit Platonism, although one should give full weight to the implications of light, warmth, and vitality in the last line, and of the immediacy of the effect the poet's power has on 'the wise'. But the confidence in the earlier images of flaming arrows and of springing seeds is here replaced by images rather of infiltration and insinuation, and the octet, with its other image of flow, strongly suggests a threat to the poet himself. If the river not only preserves, but augments its flow 'with increasing might', it can keep its blue waters 'fresh for many a mile' in the middle of the 'green salt sea'. It is hard to know how far Tennyson wishes us to push his simile, and how far, too, his 'many a mile' might be dictated by rhyme, or how far it is meant as positive or negative, for all rivers at last lose their identity in the sea, their fresh, blue, life-sustaining water merged into the green salt sea. By any interpretation, the simile conveys a strong sense of a vast environment, cold and barren, antagonistic to the 'strength of spirit, full and free' of the poet, who must pray for the power, for the preservation of his original impulse and, one feels, of his identity. The shift of similes from the river in the octet to the gulf stream in the sestet rather confuses matters, especially for the literal minded, but if we forget oceanography, geology, and the like, and consider the images independently, they cease to be incompatible. The river, carrying its purity and life-giving qualities into the alien element of the ocean, is matched by the flowing gulf stream carrying its warmth and life into the alien Northern seas. The simplicity and directness of the style and diction are notable, even if the sonnet is not faultless.

The experiments in stanza form continue. The most extreme in the degree of technical difficulty it imposes on the poet is that of *The Lady of Shalott*, where the demand for successive rhymes quadruple and triple, with two single-line refrains and short octosyllabic lines allowing little room for juggling the syntax, sets what might seem an impossible problem for the poet to solve. It is not surprising that in this first version Tennyson fails to solve it. In the first stanza he shows a kind of bravado in choice of rhyme-sound:

> On either side the river lie
> Long fields of barley and of rye,
> That clothe the wold and meet the sky;
> And through the field the road runs by
>> To many-towered Camelot;
> The yellow-leavèd waterlily,
> The green-sheathèd daffodilly,
> Tremble in the water chilly,
>> Round about Shalott.

'Lie' offers a wide choice of rhymes, but 'lily' forces him to hunt for them. Elsewhere he is brilliantly and unexpectedly successful, as in Part III, with 'eaves', 'sheaves', 'leaves', 'greaves', 'weather', 'leather', 'feather', 'together', all brought in perfectly naturally, and seeming simply to drop into place in the verse. Then at the very end of the poem he collapses catastrophically:

> They crossed themselves, their stars they blest,
> Knight, minstrel, abbot, squire and guest.
> There lay a parchment on her breast,
> That puzzled more than all the rest,
>> The wellfed wits at Camelot.
> *'The web was woven curiously,*
> *The charm is broken utterly,*
> *Draw near and fear not – this is I,*
>> *The Lady of Shalott.'*

It would be hard to compose a more disastrous anticlimax to the poem. However the wits were fed, what could they make of the message on the parchment? They know nothing of the Lady, nothing of the web or of the charm. The guest is obviously there to provide the rhyme, as is the lame third line; the rhymes 'curiously', 'utterly', 'this is I' are singularly awkward. It is as if all the poet's power had suddenly slackened, and he could hardly bother to shape the last stanza with all its technical difficulties.

Another poem using a stanza demanding multiple successive rhyme is *Fatima* (which in 1832 had no title, but an epigraph from Sappho). This uses a seven-line octosyllabic stanza rhymed *aaaabbb*. Perhaps because this is entirely lyrical, a song of passion, perhaps also because Tennyson chooses his rhyme sounds with more caution (and uses a spelling-rhyme of 'brow' with 'know', 'below', and 'blow') and because he does not limit the syntactical units within which he can manoeuvre by inserted refrains, he meets no serious difficulties with the rhyme. The freedom of the lyric mode is well illustrated in the first stanza:

> O Love, Love, Love! O withering might!
> O sun, that at thy noonday height
> Shudderest when I strain my sight,
> Throbbing through all thy heat and light,
>   Lo, falling from my constant mind,
>   Lo, parched and withered, deaf and blind,
> I whirl like leaves in roaring wind.

The freedom to move from image to image extends the range of vocabulary from which to choose a rhyme. Love in the abstract is invoked, properly associated with 'might'; the adjective 'withering' not only draws great emphasis by its apparent paradox: Love which is the principle of life and growth, the *Venus genetrix* of Lucretius, has power which can also wither and destroy; 'withering' also prepares for the shift from personification to symbol: the sun also vivifies and parches. The image of the sun then naturally produces the rhymes 'height', 'night', and 'light'. For the required new triple rhyme, the mode again shifts, to direct rather than figurative language, which allows the speaker to refer to her 'constant mind' and describe her state as 'deaf and blind'. But the sixth line also picks up the sun image again in 'parched and withered', preparing for the final line, with its dry leaves in 'roaring wind'. The stanza demonstrates very clearly how syntax and imagery function in a tight stanza form. Another good demonstration is provided by the fourth stanza (which becomes the fifth in the 1842 version):

> The wind sounds like a silver wire,
> And from beyond the noon a fire
> Is poured upon the hills, and higher
> The hills stoop down in their desire;
>   And, isled in sudden seas of light,
>   My heart, pierced through with fierce delight,
> Bursts into blossom in his sight.

It is clear that the same sort of analysis as that of the first stanza shows the same techniques. *Fatima* is by no means one of Tennyson's triumphs; *The Lady of Shalott*, even with the jarring imperfections of its 1832 version, still conveys much more sense of power and excitement. This is because the diction and images of *Fatima*, with a few exceptions like the 'silver wire' above, are adequate in an expected sort of way, generally conventional; they do not 'surprise by a fine excess'. Nor are there lines which surprise by an unexpected richness or strength of tonality. The problem Tennyson sets himself in both poems is not satisfactorily solved in either: in the first a theme and development of real power struggles unsuccessfully with the technical problems; in the second the technical problems are solved but no real poetic vitality is infused.

There are many other experiments in the 1832 volume: *The Sisters* and *The May Queen* are further examples of modifications of elements of the ballad tradition, with formulaic repetitions, refrains, and swinging metres, the latter in a form of the old fifteener couplet. At least eight of the poems are in octosyllabics, which are made to move at a great variety of speeds, from *allegretto* in *Rosalind* and *My Rosalind* (the first using stopped, the second unstopped octosyllabics) to *largo* in the quatrains of 'To J. S.' The final quatrains of this last poem offer a very fine example of Tennyson's growing power in the slow octosyllabic line, using extremely simple diction, with a high proportion of monosyllables, to give a stately movement of immense dignity, reinforced by magnificent tonalities:

> Sleep sweetly, tender heart, in peace:
> Sleep, holy spirit, blessèd soul,
> While the stars burn, the moons increase,
> And the great ages onward roll.
>
> Sleep till the end, true soul and sweet,
> Nothing comes to thee new or strange.
> Sleep full of rest from head to feet;
> Lie still, dry dust, secure of change.

The quiet melody of the first two lines swells out with the changes of the great sustained vowels – stars, burn, moons, crease, great, ages – and adjacent retarding long accents; then the quiet, light, slow movement returns, gently retarding to the last line, with its short staccato phrases, 'lie still', 'dry dust', separated by pauses, to the affirmative *coda*, lingering on the lengths of '*secure*' and '*change*'. This shows a new kind of mastery of tonality and movement.

There are other poems, like *Oenone* and *The Lotos-Eaters*, which show a further development of the earlier kinds of tonal richness; we shall have occasion to discuss them later, in another context.

One other poem calls for some examination here, *The Palace of Art*. In recent times it has attracted a great deal of attention from critics, not so much because of its poetic techniques, as because its theme seems to support one of the main theories about Tennyson's psychological and poetic development. This theory holds that during his time at Cambridge, the poet was torn between two conflicting impulses: an impulse towards withdrawal into 'Art for art's sake', and an impulse towards what modern jargon calls 'commitment', towards recognizing the social function of poetry and the poet. As we have seen, explicit manifestos setting forth the poet's nature and purpose appear in Tennyson's early poems, in *The Poet*, and in the prefatory sonnet to the 1832 volume. These affirm the poet as seer and guide, whose task is to apprehend truth and, by conveying it in its full vitality to ordinary men, enlighten and emancipate them. In arguing that Tennyson feels also a strong temptation to reject this social purpose, critics rely heavily for evidence on their interpretation of *The Palace of Art*, supported by their interpretations of *The Lotos-Eaters*, *Tithonus*, and *The Lady of Shalott*. For external evidence, they quote the remark made by R. C. Trench, remembered by Tennyson and recorded in the *Memoir* by his son Hallam: 'Tennyson, we cannot live in Art', and Tennyson's comment on this in relation to *The Palace of Art*: 'This poem is the embodiment of my own belief that the Godlike life is with man and for man.' Since we are concerned with Tennyson's development as a poet and artist, it seems necessary to make some comment on this popular critical theory, particularly since our examination of his technical development has so far put the whole emphasis on what might be thought of as 'Art for Art's sake'.

It must be recognized at the outset that there is some truth in the theory. Tennyson was very sensitive to criticism, and the relatively harsh review of the 1830 volume by Wilson and the contemptuously brutal review of the 1832 one by Croker wounded him deeply, and no doubt made him feel like withdrawing into the recesses of his own mind. But, even granting his sensitivity, Tennyson was by no means a fragile character. As one of his best and most recent critics, John Pettigrew, has noted in his little book, *Tennyson, The Early Poems*, 'Perennially fascinating is the extent to which "Tennysonian" poetry and Tennyson's personality seem to be at odds, essentially to complement rather than to reflect each other – often almost as though the gruff, very strong and masculine poet were extending and even completing himself in the creation of the delicate, the fragile, and the feminine.' Comparison with Keats, so often invited in a study of Tennyson, is relevant here, for Keats shows the same strong masculinity and inner strength, and the same complementary qualities in his poetry. It would be easy, in fact, to interpret poems like the nightingale ode, *La Belle Dame sans Merci, The Eve of Saint Agnes*, and several others, in precisely the same psychological fashion as the poems of Tennyson. Keats is, like Tennyson, aware of the attractiveness of escape, of retreat from a world of suffering, cruelty, and death into a world of the idyllic imagination. But, again like Tennyson, he knows the impossibility of escape, even on 'the viewless wings of poetry'. This is the point of Keats's poems. And this, I think, is the point of Tennyson's poems too.

It often seems to be assumed that Trench was rebuking Tennyson in his remark, or that they had been having a serious discussion about whether one *could* 'live in Art'. It is equally possible that they were entirely in agreement from the first, that they had been discussing the impossibility of 'living in Art', and that Trench summed up their attitudes in his neat phrase, which Tennyson remembered. There is no ambiguity about Tennyson's comment, 'the Godlike life is with man and for man', since there is no ambiguity about his idea of what is the Godlike life. It is not a life which imitates the Epicurean gods, 'careless of mankind'. And the one central theme which links *The Palace of Art, The Lotos-Eaters, Oenone*, and *Tithonus* is the rejection of the Epicurean view of what is 'godlike'.

> I built my soul a lordly pleasure-house,
>   Wherein at ease for aye to dwell.
> I said, 'O Soul, make merry and carouse,
>   Dear soul, for all is well.'
>
> And 'while the world runs round and round,' I said,
>   'Reign thou apart, a quiet king,
> Still as, while Saturn whirls, his steadfast shade
>   Sleeps on his luminous ring.'

The 'pleasure-house' is like the Epicurean abode of the gods described by the mariners in *The Lotos-Eaters*, where the gods lie, careless of mankind, looking down unfeeling and uncomprehending on human misery and strife.

The soul in her palace of art rejoices,

> 'O God-like isolation which art mine,
>> I can but count thee perfect gain,
> What time I watch the darkening droves of swine
>> That range on yonder plain.

> 'In filthy sloughs they roll a prurient skin,
>> They graze and wallow, breed and sleep;
> And oft some brainless devil enters in,
>> And drives them to the deep.'

In both poems there is a powerful and pervasive irony. The soul in *The Palace of Art*, and the mariners in *The Lotos-Eaters*, in their wish to become 'godlike', that is, to become like the Epicurean gods, secure in their pleasures and 'careless of mankind', seek to renounce their humanity. But their very words ironically show the impossibility. 'No man is an island'; no human being can by willing it isolate himself. The palace, it will be noted, is as much castle as palace, a carefully constructed isolation ward; the mariners' island is literally an island. But the security and isolation of the Epicurean gods depend upon the fact that they are not human, and have never been human. They are not careless of mankind because they choose or will not to care; they have no conception of what it is to be human, or to suffer. The anguished prayers of suffering humanity are meaningless to them, not because they have hardened their hearts, but because they have no knowledge of suffering. But the soul and the mariners know humanity and know suffering. The soul is not careless of mankind; she expresses anger and loathing as she speaks of the 'darkening droves of swine'. The mariners likewise cannot be 'careless'; to them the story of man is 'an ancient tale of wrong'; man is an 'ill-used race', doomed to 'enduring toil', afterwards 'to perish' and perhaps 'to suffer endless anguish'. The very phrases deny the effort at isolation; they are the words of men protesting man's lot. The lines ring with resentful envy of the Epicurean gods and with indignation on behalf of oppressed man. The soul in her palace also reveals her inescapable humanity:

Lest she should fail and perish utterly,
    God, before whom ever lie bare
The abysmal deeps of Personality,
    Plagued her with sore despair.

God here is, of course, not the Epicurean sort of god, careless of
mankind, but Tennyson's Christian God, caring for and understanding mankind. 'Personality' here, with its capital letter, is the
mystery (as Tennyson always sees it) of the human individuality
with its freedom of will and choice – the 'main-miracle' he calls it
in *De Profundis*, the poem on the birth of his son, Hallam, 'this
main-miracle, that thou art thou, With power on thine own act
and on the world'.

If then, as I have argued, the theme of *The Palace of Art* and of
the other poems associated with it is the impossibility of dis-
engaging oneself from one's own humanity (except perhaps by
becoming *less*, rather than *more* than human), and hence a rejection
of the Epicurean gods as the model to be imitated, why is it a
palace of *Art*? What has *art* to do with a theme which is basically
one about total patterns of life and how it must be lived? This is
the central question from which all the problems and ambiguities
of interpretation of the poem have arisen. And they arise because
of the ambiguities in the concept of Art itself. At the one level, as
in Keats's nightingale ode, art (or poesy) is the world of the
imagination seen as an unreal world distinguished from and
opposed to the world of actuality. In another aspect, Art is a
product, the works produced by artists, to be contemplated by
others. From the artist's point of view, Art is a creative activity, a
making, as the general word 'poesy' suggests, and the making is
active in the sense of constantly demanding choice and decision
and energy.

The kind of Art to be found in the Palace of Art is rather
peculiar. It is not of the first sort, substituting for actuality a
fictitious and attractive world of the imagination. The palace
itself is unreal, in the sense that it and its details are all chosen as
symbols, or as parts of an allegory, rather than as samples of
actual architecture. But the works of Art it contains, we are told,
are 'each a perfect whole From living Nature', 'Not less than
truth designed' (This last phrase was not in the 1832 version, but
it simply emphasizes the gist of the other words); even where the
subject is legendary, it is presented, not as something opposed to

41

Nature, but something 'which the supreme Caucasian mind carved out of nature for itself . . . not less than life, designed'. Human history, 'cycles of the human tale', representations of human thought and thinkers, poets, philosophers, systems of religion, and of science – what the Art in the palace presents is something like the totality of human experience, of all that man has seen, and thought, and done. This is Art as an imitation of nature, and especially of human nature, not Art as an escape from nature: all the beauty of reality is there, but so is the horror. It is as if some infinitely productive artist had succeeded in capturing the whole of reality, the whole truth of nature, man, the universe, in works of Art. Two things, however, strike us. The only mentions of an artist, a maker, a poet, come indirectly: the poets representative of poetry, Milton, Shakespeare, Dante, Homer, are described as 'wise men', like the philosophers, Plato and Bacon, 'godlike', 'the wise', 'large-browed', 'the first of those who know'. And the designs are 'wrought', 'carved out of nature', 'designed'. The artist is, then, not only the craftsman but the wise seer. But the emphasis throughout is not on the artist, but on the works and the soul for whom the palace is built. And as we grasp the significance of the comprehensiveness of the works as a record, an imitation, and recognize that this collection of Art is indeed presented as a microcosm, as a representation of the whole universe of nature and man, we are struck by a second recognition – that for this soul all of it is bereft of its usual meanings and emotions: that none of this Art is performing its usual function. It is Art made by human beings *for* human beings; it is wisdom acquired with pain and toil by human beings to enlighten and solace other human beings; but for the soul in her palace it has no human relevance whatsoever. One of the most familiar of Tennysonian doctrines, and indeed of Christian doctrines (central, for example, in the thought of Milton, or of Browning, to choose only two very obvious examples) is that the essence of human action, the essence of human nature, lies in the exercise of the will in choice. This is what is emphatically absent here in the soul. Plato and Bacon both offer wisdom, but as founders of the two great and opposed traditions of philosophy, they offer incompatible systems of wisdom. The true human task, as Tennyson would see it, is to use their wisdom in an attempt to see further, to choose, and to act by choice. Wisdom is for action, not for passivity. What we have in the palace, then, is Art which does not escape from life but presents it wholly; but for the soul within the palace this Art, in an important sense, ceases to be Art, losing its relevance to the reality and to the human life and world it presents. *The Palace of Art* has then from the first a powerful irony: in Tennyson's terms it is a palace of non-Art. At the end of the poem, when isolation becomes to the soul not 'godlike' but dreadful, when she has understood that her own selfhood depends on a relationship to a larger whole, and that isolation is annihilation, she descends to the valley to become one with humankind. When, as she hopes, she returns 'with others' to the palace, the Art will have a new meaning to her; it will be true Art to her, full of the music of humanity, joyous and sad, comic and tragic, beautiful and ugly – of the humanity she has re-accepted. It is the contrast between the meaninglessness of the Art to the soul in her palace before her descent into the agony of facing the truth, and the full meaning it will have on her return (which it already has for the reader, and for Tennyson) that creates all the power of the poem and its 'message'. The reader, unconsciously contributing, as a human being, all the human associations, emotions, and meanings from the start which the soul only will come to at the end, naturally is inclined to miss the point, especially since the narrator, the 'I' who builds the palace for the soul, throughout describes the works of art in familiar, recognizable terms of human reference, giving later the soul's peculiar response to them. There is thus an ironic contrast throughout between the points of view of 'I' and the soul, which can be and has been misleading. The poem is very subtle in its ironic techniques – one might say over-subtle – and a most ambitious experiment.

The stanza form represents another of Tennyson's technical experiments. The basic pattern is that of an alternate quatrain, with lines of ten, eight, ten, and six syllables respectively. The shortening of the second and fourth lines, especially the reduction of the fourth to little more than half of the third, produces a strong effect of stopping, and makes the stanza a very static one. Tennyson accepts and exploits the static effect by generally avoiding any run-on from stanza to stanza; relatively few stanzas end with any other punctuation than a full stop. Much of his material, consequently, is formed into a series of neat little sketches or vignettes, carefully contained within the stanza form.

The skill with which this is for the most part achieved marks the poet's growing mastery of composition within a demanding form. To secure movement, and to bind the static little quatrains into larger verse paragraphs, he relies mainly on syntax and rhetorical patterns, which in effect vary the fullness of the full stop. The technique can be most conveniently illustrated from the revised version of 1842, since this text is more readily available. In stanzas six to nine (lines 21 to 36), the 'four courts' and the 'flood of fountain-foam' of stanza six are referred to in the next stanza, as 'the cool green courts' and the 'spouted fountain-floods', and picked up again in stanza nine, 'From those four jets'. The method, using very specific references back to clear antecedents, gives a lucid flow of related ideas, making for a strong and smooth organized flow. What are virtually long catalogues of items, each contained within its stanza, are given unity and movement by similar rhetorical techniques: the landscapes of lines 65 following, 'One seemed', 'One moved', 'And one', 'And one', 'And one', 'And one', 'Nor these alone'; the portrayals of religious themes (lines 93 following), in eight stanzas each beginning 'Or', again followed by 'Nor these alone', show the obvious but effective method. The static stanza retains its slow tempo, but the rhetorical devices keep the large structure coherent and dynamic.

Given such a restrictive stanza and such apparently mechanical methods as repetition and parallelism, it would seem difficult for the poet to avoid monotony through repetition of patterns within the stanza. Tennyson succeeds in giving his stanzas constant variety, by changing syntax, diction, tonality, and tempo within the stanzas. A few examples, again from the text of 1842, will illustrate. Consider the sound and movement of successive final short lines in almost any group of stanzas:

> Well-pleased, from room to room.
> And change of my still soul.
> His wreathèd bugle-horn.
> Lit with a low large moon.
> Beneath the windy wall.
> With shadow-streaks of rain.
> And hoary to the wind.

No two have the same metrical movement, or tempo, or tonal

pattern. The diction varies from the very common, even domestic,
language of the first, to the more poetic fourth, sixth and seventh
lines, the very romantic 'wreathèd bugle-horn' of the third, the
matter-of-fact but evocative 'beneath the windy wall', and the
simple but highly suggestive and packed 'change of my still soul'.
The same sort of variety extends of course to whole stanzas.
Consider the diction of these stanzas from the 1832 version
(some omitted in 1842):

> Far off 'twas wonderful to look upon
>   Those sumptuous towers between the gleam
> Of that great foambow trembling in the sun,
>   And the argent incense-steam . . .
>
> With piles of flavorous fruits in basket-twine
>   Of gold, upheapèd, crushing down
> Musk scentèd blooms – all taste – grape, gourd or pine –
>   In bunch, or singlegrown –
>
> Our growths, and such as brooding Indian heats
>   Make out of crimson blossoms deep,
> Ambrosial pulps and juices, sweets from sweets
>   Sunchanged, when seawinds sleep . . .
>
> Regions of lucid matter taking forms,
>   Brushes of fire, hazy gleams,
> Clusters and beds of worlds, and bee-like swarms
>   Of suns, and starry streams . . .
>
> A still salt pool, locked in with bars of sand,
>   Left on the shore; that hears all night
> The plunging seas draw backward from the land
>   Their moon-led waters white . . .
>
> And death and life she hated equally,
>   And nothing saw, for her despair,
> But dreadful time, dreadful eternity,
>   No comfort anywhere . . .

Consider also the syntactical contrasts in the structure of these
quatrains and of the following (from the 1842 text), where the
syntax is made to break the flow of the stanza:

And one, the reapers at their sultry toil.
    In front they bound the sheaves. Behind
Were realms of upland, prodigal in oil,
    And hoary to the wind.

Tennyson has obviously achieved a high degree of mastery in composing in stanzaic forms. Already his attention is moving towards further artistic problems.

CHAPTER 2

The Shape of a Poem:
'Every poem should have a shape'

❧❧❧❧❧❧

THE ten years between the publication of the 1832 volume and that of the two volumes of *Poems* in 1842, which finally established Tennyson's reputation firmly, used to be called the ten years of silence. There was a popular impression that the unfriendly reception of the earlier volumes had so discouraged the poet that he went through a period of inactivity before he could bring himself back with confidence to his task of writing. The truth is that the ten years were very active ones, in which Tennyson was not only doing a great deal of new writing, but revising, often radically, the earlier poems which still seemed promising to him. The nature of the revisions is most interesting, since in general they show a new or vastly increased awareness of the necessity of total shape and structure in a poem. It is as if he had, in the earlier poems, been so preoccupied with the technical problems we examined in the last chapter, with experiments in metrics, in tonalities, in mastering stanza forms of increasing intricacy, in discovering how to control pace and tempo, and the effects of different kinds of language, that he had devoted much less attention to what might be called the architecture of the poem. Now he makes this a main concern, and it remains so for the rest of his career. He continues, of course, his old types of experiment, trying and mastering constantly new effects of detail, but he now explores also varieties of total shape and structure. We can illustrate some of his methods by examining some of the revisions he makes in the earlier poems.

Perhaps the most radical, and certainly one of the most amazingly successful, is the surgery he performed on *The Lady of Shalott*. Some of the revisions made in this poem for 1842 are purely tonal: Tennyson particularly referred to 'kicking the geese out of the boat', that is, reducing the hissing sibilants, especially adjacent ones. In the original second stanza, for example, he wrote

> Willows whiten, aspens shiver,
> The sun beam-showers break and quiver
> In the stream that runneth ever.

There are eight sibilants in the three lines. The revised version neatly transposes 'shiver' and 'quiver', subdues the emphatic sibilants of 'sunbeam-showers' to the muted 'Little breezes dusk and shiver' (brilliantly improving the image at the same time), and puts 'wave' in place of 'stream'. There are a number of revisions of this sort, to improve tonality and tighten the sense. But far more important are the revisions for structural tightening. The first of these is in the third stanza, which in 1832 began

> The little isle is all inrailed
> With a rose-fence, and overtrailed
> With roses: by the marge unhailed
> The shallop flitteth silken-sailed . . .

It was also, in 1832, placed after the stanza about the reapers, so that stanzas three and four of 1832 become interchanged in 1842. The effect of the move and of detailed changes is worth noting.

The original opening stanza had set up a brilliant contrast between the colour and movement of the world outside, where road and river run down to Camelot, and 'up and down the people go,' and the cold immobility of the 'Four gray walls, and four gray towers' of the 'silent isle'. But this powerful effect is blurred in the 1832 text by the detail that follows. The reaper, in 1832, 'hears *her* ever chanting cheerly, Like an angel, singing clearly'. In 1842, the reapers only hear *a song*. And the description of the island quoted above, which was followed by a sharply detailed description of the Lady:

> A pearl garland winds her head:
> She leaneth on a velvet bed,
> Fully royally apparellèd . . .

is now removed. In place of the rich visual detail which, by allowing us to see the Lady and her bower as vividly and as clearly as the outside world, destroyed the contrast and fused her and her island into visual unity with the outside, we now have three rhetorical questions, to all of which the answer is the same:

48

> But who hath seen her wave her hand?
> Or at the casement seen her stand?
> Or is she known in all the land,
>   The Lady of Shalott?

She is now a legend and a voice, unseen, unknown. The reaper cannot know that he hears *her* voice: he hears *a voice* and attributes it to 'the fairy Lady'. The towers now stand in their grayness, overlooking a space of flowers, but the island itself is no longer a place itself of colour and growth, 'over-trailed with roses'. No one sees any sign of life there, the shallop flits by 'unhailed'; there is only that mysterious song heard by the reapers.

The middle of the poem, Parts II and III, needed much less revision, but here again the central structure is clarified and tightened.

> No time hath she to sport and play:
> A charmèd web she weaves alway.
> A curse is on her, if she stay
> Her weaving, either night or day,
>   To look down to Camelot.
> She knows not what the curse may be,
> Therefore she weaveth steadily,
> Therefore no other care hath she,
>   The Lady of Shalott.

This original loose stanza, with its abundant archaisms and its tautologies, is replaced by the tightly organized 1842 version, with its packed suggestions:

> There she weaves by night and day
> A magic web with colours gay.
> She has heard a whisper say,
> A curse is on her if she stay
>   To look down to Camelot.

And instead of the archaic but nonsensical 'Therefore', which suggests logical conclusions, we now have the more neutral 'And so'. The Lady herself now has, even to herself, the imprecision and mystery of a legend and of magic. The single phrase 'colours gay' at once suggests the connection of the web and the outside world, and in the revised second stanza of Part II this is made explicit, as it was not in 1832. Now, in the mirror 'that hangs before her all the year, Shadows of the world appear'. The sharp contrast established by the revisions now allows us to see the bright outside world, the gay figures moving up and down the road and the river, part of a whole world of colour and life, and to see also the gray room inside the gray walls and gray towers, and the mysterious and undefined figure of the Lady, motionless except for her eyes and her fingers, placed before the two little areas of colour in her gray world: the moving colour of the 'shadows' in the mirror, the static colour of her tapestry. The strong climax of Part II, '"I am half-sick of shadows," said The Lady of Shalott', now strikes with ten-fold force.

Part III was originally the most perfect of the poem, and needed very little revision. One significant little change, in accordance with those in earlier stanzas, is from 'green Shalott' in stanza three to 'still Shalott'. The two refrains before, 'Beside remote Shalott', already emphasized the separation of the island; 'green', like the opening description, attributed life to the island as well as to its surroundings.

Part IV was by far the worst of the original poem. It again destroyed the mystery, and with it all the immense suggestiveness of the poem, by concrete visual description of the Lady. The original second stanza, full of affected archaisms, padding, and rhyme dictation, read:

> A cloudwhite crown of pearl she dight.
> All raimented in snowy white
> That loosely flew, (her zone in sight,
> Clasped with one blinding diamond bright,)
>> Her wide eyes fixed on Camelot.
> Though the squally eastwind keenly
> Blew, with folded arms serenely
> By the water stood the queenly
>> Lady of Shalott.

This awkward stanza mercifully disappears completely, and description is reduced to the superb suggestions of the third stanza:

> Lying, robed in snowy white
> That loosely flew to left and right –
> The leaves upon her falling light –
> Through the noises of the night
>> She floated down to Camelot:
> And as the boat-head wound along
> The willowy hills and fields among,
> They heard her singing her last song,
>> The Lady of Shalott.

This stanza is of special interest as a sign of Tennyson's new kind of artistry, because it reached its final form through the discarding of five of the best lines in the original poem. A death song naturally suggested to the young poet the dying swan, and the first part of this stanza in 1832 read:

> As when to sailors while they roam
> By creeks and outfalls far from home,
> Rising and dropping with the foam,
> From dying swans wild warblings come,
> Blown shoreward; so to Camelot . . .

These tonally beautiful and romantically suggestive lines the mature poet drops entirely from the poem. Tightness of structure demands no excursions, however beautiful, into epic simile here.

The final stanza, which we glanced at in its dreadful bathos earlier, is replaced by an absolute triumph:

> Who is this? and what is here?
> And in the lighted palace near
> Died the sound of royal cheer;
> And they crossed themselves for fear,
>   All the knights of Camelot:
> But Lancelot mused a little space;
> He said, 'She has a lovely face;
> God in his mercy lend her grace,
>   The Lady of Shalott.'

The sense of mystery is preserved in the questions, and the sense of something strange and to be feared in the effects on the palace and the knights. The world of Shalott, the gray world, intrudes into the joyous, active world of Camelot for a moment, and grips it with its stillness. Lancelot alone feels anything but fear for himself; he alone, the unconscious cause of her death, feels pity for her and her beauty, and prays, not for himself, but for her. The power of this conclusion, with its fine irony, is enhanced by the diction, which becomes here extremely simple and direct.

The contrast between the two versions of the poem is not simply that between incompetence and competence. Primarily it is that between an infirm and a firm grasp of the poem's structure. It seems evident that in the 1832 version Tennyson is concentrating on the technical problems posed by the difficult stanza form. As far as a general mode of treatment of the theme is concerned, he seems to see it only as a medieval legend, attractively Romantic in its elements of magic and fairylore, suitable for a rich pictorial development. He accordingly develops it through elaboration of visual description. But at the same time, a sense of the theme central to the 1842 version is in the back of his mind, and appears here and there in the poem. Two things happen in the revision: he gets complete control of the stanza form, so that it no longer dictates to him, no longer forces him into weak padding or into irrelevancies, and he sees very clearly what his poem is about, and how to shape it as a total form.

Another illustration of the same sort of mature craftsmanship and artistic insight can be seen in the first stanza of *Mariana in the South*. In some ways this is an even better illustration than *The Lady of Shalott*, since the original stanza is an excellent one.

> Behind the barren hills upsprung
>   With pointed rocks against the light,
> The crag sharpshadowed overhung
>   Each glaring creek and inlet bright.
> Far, far, one lightblue ridge was seen,
>   Looming like baseless fairyland;
>   Eastward a slip of burning sand,
> Dark-rimmed with sea, and bare of green.
> Down in the dry salt-marshes stood
>   That house dark latticed. Not a breath
>   Swayed the sick vineyard underneath,
> Or moved the dusty southernwood.
>   'Madonna,' with melodious moan
> Sang Mariana, night and morn,
>   'Madonna! lo! I am all alone,
>   Love-forgotten and love-forlorn!'

The landscape is set out here almost with the care of a topographical painting: the eye starts in the distance, with the pointed backlit line of mountains dominated by the crag, sharpshadowed in the dry hard light. The sun glares from the water of creek and inlet, between the crag and the sea. Beyond, barely visible above the water, is the light blue ridge of a distant further range of mountains, bases lost in the blue haze. To the left is the sea, dark against the pale glare of the narrow sandy shore. In the foreground lie the dry salt-marshes and the house in its dying vineyard. The scene, viewed from background to the near distance, is vividly realized; the actual landscape which it describes, seen by Tennyson and Arthur Hallam in the summer of 1830 on the northern edge of the Pyrenees, is so emphatically present to the poet's eye that he describes it minutely and faithfully as he saw it. What struck him first in the actual scene is what strikes every Englishman who first sees the eastern slopes of the Rocky Mountains: in the thin, dry air, the edges of mountains ten or twenty miles away are as sharply defined, and their colours are as hard and undimmed, as if they were close at hand. This first powerful impression of a blazing clarity in objects always softened by distance in the English air dominates the description. As Arthur Hallam said of the poem, 'the portraiture of the scenery is most faithful'. So intent is the poet on the portraiture that he uses twelve lines before the refrain in this opening stanza, instead of the eight he has chosen as the normal for the poem. It seems evident that his real compulsion in the first stanza is to render the landscape in complete detail, before emphasizing its significance to the theme of the poem, and the details took up eight lines before he got to Mariana's house and its setting. The result is a brilliant piece of landscape description, with the poet's eye sharply on the object, and noting the composition of its elements. But his concentration is on what is important to an accurate description, not on what is essential to the theme of the poem.

The skill with which he remodels the stanza is evident:

> With one black shadow at its feet,
>   The house through all the level shines,
> Close-latticed to the brooding heat,
>   And silent in its dusty vines:
> A faint-blue ridge upon the right,
>   An empty river-bed before,
>   And shallows on a distant shore,
> In glaring sand and inlets bright.
>   But 'Ave Mary', made she moan,
>   And 'Ave Mary', night and morn,
> And 'Ah', she sang, 'to be all alone,
>   To live forgotten, and love forlorn.'

The eye now is made to move from foreground to background, and what dominates the landscape is the house with its shadow, the only black shadow in a great level glare. The background which dominated the earlier description is now reduced to setting, and sketched in rapidly. All the elements are still there, and the composition of elements is the same, but the shift of focus from the sharp definition of the distant ridge, the creeks and the sea to the nearby house turns the whole view from one of the Pyrenees seen against the light with incidental foreground to one of a house in a sun-drenched plain with the Pyrenees as background. Quite small verbal changes in the new version produce very large effects. 'Shines' in the second line conveys at once the dazzling brilliance of a white house on a dry plain, its whiteness intensified by the depth of its shadow. 'Close-latticed', replacing 'dark latticed', is reinforced by 'brooding', to suggest the defensive: the heat surrounds the house like an enemy, trying to force entry. The language is still strongly visual, but no longer simply so. It now carries a double function as symbol: the landscape is still a brilliantly drawn landscape, but it is also a symbolic one. The sun, the light, and the heat are felt as sensations, but also apprehended as symbols: the sun can bring growth but also destruction; here the vineyard, that powerful symbol of life, is dying under the dust. The power of the opening lines is reinforced by the tonality and metrics; the impact of the visual image of the house and its associated symbolism are strongly aided by the vigour of stress and tonality of 'one black shadow'; the length of the second line, with its long vowels, and the quiet tonality of its liquid and sibilant consonants, by a kind of onomatopoeia suggests the endless stretch of the plain. The incomplete syntax of lines five to eight supports the sense of quick rough sketching of the background and by contrast lends further strength to the opening quatrain. The changes in the refrain are brilliant: 'Ave Mary' is more recognizably a prayer than 'Madonna', and the shift from 'I am all alone' to 'to be all alone' generalizes Mariana's condition to the universal. And in the last line, a simple vowel change doubles the meaning: to *live* forgotten, and *love* forlorn.' The grammatical change in the same line from adjectival 'love-forgotten and love-forlorn' to the verbal 'to live' and 'to love' is also a very happy one. The conventional ballad archaism 'made she moan' keeps the suggestion in the refrain of the ballad tradition, while being less tritely conventional, perhaps, than the 'melodious moan' of 1832.

Other revisions elsewhere in the poem are of the same general type. In the third stanza,

> She moved her lips, she prayed alone,
>   She praying disarrayed and warm
>   From slumber, deep her wavy form
> In the darklustrous mirror shone . . .

becomes in 1842

> Complaining, 'Mother, give me grace
>   To help me of my weary load.'
>   And on the liquid mirror glowed
> The clear perfection of her face.

Distracting specific description is again brilliantly reduced to powerfully suggestive general description, and the dramatic given prime emphasis.

Similarly, the original fourth stanza was given over to a detailed description of Mariana's dream. In the revised version, this is again reduced to powerful general terms, and to four lines, which allow the next four lines to set the contrast of actuality:

> Nor bird would sing, nor lamb would bleat,
>   Nor any cloud would cross the vault,
> But day increased from heat to heat,
>   On stony drought and steaming salt;
> Till now at noon she slept again,
>   And seemed knee-deep in mountain grass,
>   And heard her native breezes pass,
> And runlets babbling down the glen.

Here again, then, as in *The Lady of Shalott*, Tennyson has moved from a delight in sharply visualized description for purely pictorial effect towards a compressed style which subordinates description to the needs of his theme and structure. At the same time, he has acquired a virtually complete mastery over the complex stanza.

Some experimental structures begun earlier are further developed. The finest example is *The Lotos-Eaters*. The form of this poem, in its final 1842 version, is highly unusual. Tennyson had often combined two metrical forms in one poem: in *The Hesperides*, for example, he began with blank verse and then moved into a free rhymed choric song. The first version of *The Lotos-Eaters* followed a similar pattern, opening with five Spenserian stanzas, then moving to a series of choric songs. In 1842 the long final choric song is re-written so that after an opening couplet it proceeds in triplet rhyme, the line length rapidly settling into almost regular fifteeners. The effect now is of a regular metrical movement at the opening and at the close, with the irregular choric movements in the centre. A 'sandwich' structure is not, of course, uncommon in music and in poetry, but it is more usual in an ABA form of this sort to have a close similarity in pattern in the two A parts. Here the Spenserian stanzas and the fifteener triplets make a strong contrast. Another peculiarity is that the metrical structure is not made to coincide with the thematic structure. The final chorus, metrically distinct from the other choruses, is not marked off as separate, and indeed flows smoothly from the choruses before. This is obvious enough. But the opening Spenserian stanzas, which by their closed metrical forms and typographical separation suggest self-containment, are not actually self-contained. Thematically, the first two lines of the opening stanza, giving the action and speech of the unnamed Ulysses, stand in isolation from the rest of the poem. They remind us at the outset of the epic narrative, and especially of its ending: we are ironically aware throughout of the strong will of Ulysses, the spirit expressed in the trumpeting of the first word, 'Courage!' We know that when the time comes, that hard voice will ring out again and the mariners will troop back to the oars. Their listless attempt to decide to make no decisions, to will not to will, to renounce all aspiration but the passive search for pleasure, has no chance against the single-minded determination and iron will for action of their leader. The word 'Courage' echoes ironically behind all the languid tones of the chorus. The last of the Spenserian stanzas is similarly split by the thematic structure. Its sixth line concludes the theme begun by the third line of the first stanza:

> In the afternoon they came upon a land
> In which it seemèd always afternoon . . .
> They sat them down upon the yellow sand,
> Between the sun and moon upon the shore;
> And sweet it was to dream of Fatherland,
> Of child, and wife, and slave; but evermore
> Most weary seemed the sea, weary the oar,
> Weary the wandering fields of barren foam.

The lines move here to a finish: the exposition is complete. The last three lines of the stanza move into the development of the choruses; the song begins within the stanza, and flows over its ending:

> Then some one said, 'We will return no more!'
> And all at once they sang, 'Our island home
> Is far beyond the wave; we will no longer roam.'
> There is sweet music here that softer falls
> Than petals from blown roses on the grass . . .

The metrical pattern does not, then, in this poem reinforce the thematic one by coinciding with it, as is the more usual case. It must function, not logically by the subject matter, but musically or tonally by the sound. And if the poem is read aloud with an attentive ear, it is evident that the metrical forms do in fact serve musical purposes.

After the *forte* and *con brio* opening two lines, the slow movement of the Spenserian stanza – made even more languid by Tennyson's exploiting the extra length of the final lines: 'Along the cliff to fall and pause and fall did seem', 'up-clomb the shadowy pine above the woven copse', and by his repetitions of long vowels: 'And deep-asleep he seemed, yet all awake' – continues its regular pace until the reader's ear is attuned to the tempo, which will remain pulsing slowly in his memory behind the varied *tempi* of the choruses. The choruses, with their free line-lengths, and consequently varied spacing of rhyme-sounds, introduce slight *rallentandos* and *accelerandos*, and muted *agitato* movements, all heard as counterpointed against the fundamental slow beat of the opening. Little brittle phrases can disturb the slow mellifluous flow of the more narcotic passages:

> Why are we weighed upon with heaviness,
> And utterly consumed with sharp distress . . .
> Portions and parcels of the dreadful Past . . .
> Let what is broken so remain.
> The Gods are hard to reconcile:
> 'Tis hard to settle order once again . . .
> Trouble on trouble, pain on pain . . .

The slow movement and its smooth tonality are reasserted from time to time in these choruses by regular lines in clusters, echoing the Spenserian pattern.

The final chorus changes the rhythmic movement, and by its long sustained passage of fifteener triplets, establishes what might seem a paradoxically energetic thrust. The length of the lines and the insistency of the triplet rhymes make this also a slow movement, but it has a very different tonal and metrical quality from that of the opening Spenserian stanzas.

> Blight and famine, plague and earthquake, roaring deeps
> and fiery sands,
> Clanging fights, and flaming towns, and sinking ships,
> and praying hands.

These are not lines expressive of lassitude, they are marked by strong indignation over man's lot, a measured, stately, and angry denunciation of the gods who find man's tragedy meaningless or amusing. When, at the end of the chorus, the lines lose their energy and relax and slow to a stop, the lassitude is not that of the drugged pleasure-seeker, but of the exhausted and toil-worn sufferer. The whole movement contrasts ironically with the main movement, giving emphasis to the irony of the theme. The mariners, wishing to reject their humanity and become, like the Epicurean gods, careless of mankind, are roused by their own sense of outraged human dignity to something approaching reassertion of human will. They become, in fact, closer once more to Ulysses' description of them, ready to do 'work of noble note . . . Not unbecoming men that strove with Gods'. They are again at one with mankind, awaiting only the stirring of the will, the commanding voice of their human leader.

The conclusion is prepared for by the sixth chorus, added during revision. It is filled with allusions to the epic action, to what 'the minstrel sings . . . of the ten years' war in Troy', to the 'island princes over-bold' who have eaten the mariners' substance, to the confusion in their 'little isle'. Their thoughts are strongly drawn to the past and to the future, to their exploits and great deeds, to their present duties, even as they seek excuses to escape them. They cannot cease to care, and have not ceased to care, and the lines of this chorus begin to stir with echoes of epic dignity and strength. 'Our looks are strange', they sing, 'And we should come like ghosts to trouble joy', and the reader's mind flashes to the return of Ulysses, recognized only by his dog Argo, and to his defeat of the riotous suitors of Penelope. This reminder of the epic action within which the limited scene of *The Lotos-Eaters* is set prepares for the full irony of the final chorus.

To some extent the complex ironic movement of the poem was implicit in the earlier version, just as much of the theme and structure of *The Lady of Shalott* was implicit, but not realized, in the version of 1832. The choric songs of the mariners, antiphonal in form, presenting alternately the pleasures of ease and the pains of toil, from the beginning contained a progression or movement. The emphasis is at first on the purely physical, on physical ease and physical toil. The third chorus, with its beautiful evocation of the delights of a purely vegetable existence, of the 'life of nature' as idealized in the careless career of the 'full-juiced apple', completes this stage of the theme. The next chorus very abruptly and significantly shifts attention from physical to moral in the question, 'What pleasure can we have to war with evil?' And much larger issues than mere physical pleasure are suggested by the mariners' complaint, 'All things are taken from us, and become Portions and parcels of the dreadful Past.' The view of life as a process of subtraction, of past experience as bits of oneself wrapped up, cut off, separated and abstracted, of Time nibbling away at the self, contrasts with the view of Ulysses, who sees experience as additive: 'I am a part of all that I have met.' To seek a vegetable existence, a mere physical one, is to try to separate oneself from the distinctively human in life and its experience. Time does not in fact take things from us; our past is always with us. The sixth chorus, added in revision, develops these ideas implicit in the original fourth chorus.

The form of the poem, then, superficially so static, and in parts of its development exploiting static metrical and tonal patterns, nevertheless is basically a movement, a progress, marked most openly by the contrast between the Spenserian stanzas of the opening and the long, surging triplets of the close. It is a complex and subtle structure, and a successful one.

Much less successful is the structure of *The Vision of Sin*. As its title indicates, the poem is an allegorical vision, and as such it is related, however distantly, to both *The Vision of Piers the Plowman* and *The Pilgrim's Progress*. Its theme is related to that of *The Lotos-Eaters* in that it treats of the destructive effects of the pursuit of pleasure; in Tennyson's own words, the poem 'describes the soul of a youth who has given himself up to pleasure and Epicureanism. He at length is worn out and wrapt in the mists of satiety. Afterwards he grows into a cynical old man afflicted with the "curse of nature", and joining in the Feast of Death. Then we see the landscape which symbolizes God, Law and the future life'.

The first section of the poem is of thirteen lines, heroic couplets ending with a triplet, the last line being an alexandrine. A youth is riding towards a palace-gate, his mount a horse with wings, 'that would have flown, But that his heavy rider kept him down'. He is led into the palace by 'a child of sin', 'where sat a company with heated eyes, . . . A sleepy light upon their brows and lips, . . . sitting, lying, languid shapes, By heaps of gourds, and skins of wine, and piles of grapes'. The company clearly show resemblances to the Lotos-eaters, marked by the adjectives 'sleepy' and 'languid', but 'heated eyes' suggests something other than the passivity of the Lotos-eaters, and the final line connects them rather with Bacchus than with the Epicurean gods, and hence, with the 'heated', prepares us not for the pleasures of ease and lassitude, but for the mad frenzy of the Bacchic rout, of the Maenads. And this is what the second section of the poem gives us. This is a virtuoso performance, a triumph of technique, a single sentence of thirty-two lines, moving at first slowly and hesitantly, and then, from the twelfth line (line 25 of the poem) accelerating with tremendous velocity and impetus, then dying down in the last three lines. A short extract will show the effect and how it is produced:

> . . . The strong tempestuous treble throbbed and palpitated;
> Ran its giddiest whirl of sound,
> Caught the sparkles, and in circles,
> Purple gauzes, golden hazes, liquid mazes,
> Flung the torrent rainbow round . . .
> Wheeling with precipitate paces
> To the melody, till they flew,
> Hair, and eyes, and limbs, and faces,
> Twisted hard in fierce embraces,
> Like to Furies, like to Graces,
> Dashed together in blinding dew:
> Till, killed with some luxurious agony,
> The nerve-dissolving melody
> Fluttered headlong from the sky.

The internal rhymes and near-rhymes, 'sparkles', 'circles', 'gauzes', 'hazes', 'mazes', the rapid patter of consonants in 'precipitate paces', the clustering of the rhymes, and the increasing force of the accents in trochaic pattern, all give immense impetus to the verse. Then the motion is suddenly stopped by a lengthening and slowing of the lines and by an even distribution of stress.

The third section introduces the 'landscape which symbolizes God, Law and the future life', and the 'cynical old man', leading directly into the fourth section, the song of the 'gray and gap-toothed man'. The structure of section three shows again the influence of Tennyson's experiments in sonnet and stanza forms. It is in regular pentameters, rhymed *abbab cdcd efef ghhg*. The elements of the symbolic landscape are ones that become permanent for Tennyson: a mountain-tract, from which a cataract descends ('Force is from the heights'), and above the mountains, 'far withdrawn Beyond the darkness and the cataract, God made Himself an awful rose of dawn'. This final powerful image, reminiscent of Faustus's 'See! Christ's blood streams in the firmament', offers a warning and a promise, both unheeded by the inhabitants of the palace of sin.

> God made Himself an awful rose of dawn,
> Unheeded: and detaching, fold by fold,
> From those still heights, and, slowly drawing near,
> A vapour heavy, hueless, formless, cold,
> Came floating on for many a month and year,
> Unheeded . . .

The emphatic placing of the repeated 'unheeded', and the menacing movement of the fourth line – 'heavy, hueless, formless, cold' – as the cold vapour of death engulfs the palace of sin, create a powerful piece of symbolic drama.

The last lines introduce a new symbolic landscape, that of the Wasteland:

> I saw within my head
> A gray and gap-toothed man as lean as death,
> Who slowly rode across a withered heath,
> And lighted at a ruined inn, and said . . .

And what he said makes up the long fourth section of the poem, thirty-six octosyllabic quatrains in alternate rhyme – 144 lines of the 224 line poem.

There can be little doubt that the sheer length of this section throws the poem out of balance: the song of the ruined old man goes on too long, and delays too long the return at the end to the symbolic landscape. And the tone and style of the quatrains are far from uniformly successful. Many years ago Oliver Elton dismissed them as 'in Tennyson's worst ranting style'. This is a peculiar judgement; one could as readily dismiss passages in *The Wasteland* as in T. S. Eliot's worst ranting style. But Elton's comment is not without significance. The lines are meant to be ranting, full of the shallow rhetoric of the hollow man, but the point is sufficiently made long before the stanzas cease. Nor is the kind of ranting always the same. The opening stanzas are almost like a parody of Tennyson's own *Will Waterproof's Lyrical Monologue*, and are very loosely written:

> 'Bitter barmaid, waning fast!
> See that sheets are on my bed;
> What! the flower of life is past:
> It is long before you wed.'

This is by any standard a lame quatrain. In fact the first nine quatrains could be dispensed with, although to remove the ninth would eliminate an entertaining literary anecdote, which I cannot refrain from giving here, for it too embodies a kind of criticism. The original form of the quatrain, as published in 1842, read:

> 'Fill the cup, and fill the can:
> Have a rouse before the morn:
> Every minute dies a man,
> Every minute one is born.'

Tennyson's friend Babbage, the mathematician, best known as inventor of the first successful adding machine, a man of genius and of wit, wrote Tennyson a mock-solemn letter, pointing out that the birth-rate exceeds the death-rate, and consequently suggesting as a revision:

> Every minute dies a man,
> And one and a sixteenth is born.

'The exact figures', added Babbage, 'are 1·167, but something must . . . be conceded to the laws of metre'. From 1851 on, Tennyson changed 'minute' to 'moment', a less specific time-interval.

The tenth quatrain is the first really effective one:

> 'We are men of ruined blood;
> Therefore comes it we are wise.
> Fish are we that love the mud,
> Rising to no fancy-flies.'

The following quatrains, sneering at name and fame, at friendship, virtue, religion, politics, freedom, are very pertinent to the theme and what might be called good ranting. Especially good are those on political ideals:

> 'He that roars for liberty
> Faster binds a tyrant's power;
> And the tyrant's cruel glee
> Forces on the freer hour . . .

> 'Greet her with applausive breath,
> Freedom, gaily doth she tread;
> In her right a civic wreath,
> In her left a human head . . .

> 'Drink to lofty hopes that cool –
> Visions of a perfect State:
> Drink we, last, the public fool,
> Frantic love and frantic hate . . .'

And finally,

> 'Drink to Fortune, drink to Chance,
> While we keep a little breath!
> Drink to heavy Ignorance!
> Hob-and-nob with brother Death! . .

> 'Fill the cup, and fill the can:
> Mingle madness, mingle scorn!
> Dregs of life, and lees of man:
> Yet we will not die forlorn.'

Something like ten or twelve of the best quatrains, those in particular that express familiar cynical attitudes, would have made Tennyson's point in the poem, and fulfilled the needs of its structure without throwing it out of proportion. The powerful symbolism of the final section would then have stood out more dominantly.

But in the final section there seems also to be a deficiency in structure. The symbolic landscape reappears, but below it this time is a region of death, 'men and horses pierced with worms . . . By shards and scurf of salt, and scum of dross, Old plash of rains, and refuse patched with moss'. The landscape, as symbol, speaks for itself: the wages of sin is Death. A further question can however be asked: 'Is this Death final?' To finish the poem at this point with its last line, 'God made Himself an awful rose of dawn' would have sent the reader's mind back to the earlier 'unheeded', leaving the implication that for those who do not heed, that is the end. This is not what Tennyson wishes to say. So he follows the vision of Death by these lines:

> Then some one spake: 'Behold! it was a crime
> Of sense avenged by sense that wore with time.'
> Another said, 'The crime of sense became
> The crime of malice, and is equal blame.'
> And one: 'He had not wholly quenched his power;
> A little grain of conscience made him sour.'

This discussion of the nature and relative depravity of the sin committed by the gray and gap-toothed man couched in terms of familiar distinctions, of sins of the appetites and sins of the will, of whether a remnant of conscience can be a saving grace, is actually of importance in Tennyson's theme. These are the considerations men have put forward in trying to determine whom God will save and whom He will condemn eternally. Tennyson's own view is presented in the closing lines:

> At last I heard a voice upon the slope
> Cry to the summit, 'Is there any hope?'
> To which an answer pealed from that high land,
> But in a tongue no man could understand;
> And on the glimmering limit far withdrawn
> God made Himself an awful rose of dawn.

This by implication dismisses the three separate and distinct judgements – human judgements. When man asks the question, 'Is there any hope?' an answer comes, – it is 'pealed', it rings out 'from that high land'. But it is not an answer in terms intelligible to men or translatable into human language. But he can hear that there *is* an answer, and above all, that someone is giving the answer. And this itself is a ground of hope. The final line, then, which at its first appearance in the poem conveys a symbol of both warning and promise, now is dominantly affirmative. The thematic sequence of the first section of the poem is thus clear, but the shift from symbolic landscape to the human dogmatic judgements and back to symbolic landscape is still structurally disturbing, though it is not easy to see how else Tennyson could have accomplished his purpose.

But the real failure of what comes close to being a successful poem is in the overwriting of the fourth section, and one suspects that some of the exuberance of the very young Tennyson came back to him as he wrote these easy, loose quatrains and prevailed over his growing sense of form.

CHAPTER 3

Style and Genre

🆂🆂🆂🆂🆂🆂

As he moved away from the simple exuberance of his youthful writing, and from the excitement of capturing successfully the tones and movements of all sorts of styles for the sheer delight of the writing, Tennyson turned to serious consideration of style as related to genre. This was a subject that eighteenth-century poets and critics, following the lead of Dryden, had very much concerned themselves with: What are the different sorts or kinds of poetry, and what sort of language is most appropriate to each? Their aims generally were to define the genres and also to define the style proper to each, creating a system for poetry and critics alike. The poets tended to be less rigorous in their system-making than the critics, and were prepared to invent or to recognize new genres: it was the critics rather than the poets who condemned Shakespeare for mixing comedy and tragedy; Dryden argued that he had created a new and valid kind of drama. But even granting a degree of flexibility in the acceptance and definition of genres, the dominant idea underlying their approach was that of decorum: That certain themes, styles, and kinds of diction are fitting for each kind of writing. Their persistent use of the clothes metaphor – 'language is the dress of thought' – with the accompanying sense of the different sorts of clothing suitable for a formal reception at court, for a walk in the country, or for relaxing with a few intimate friends, expresses vividly their sense of the kind of tone and method of address suitable, say, for an epic or high tragedy, for a poem of rural description, or for a familiar epistle. Just as they found comedy in an over-dressed rustic or tradesman, self-conscious in his unaccustomed finery, so they exploited the comedy of the mock-heroic, which applied 'high' style to a 'low' subject, or in burlesque, which applied 'low' style to a dignified subject. The whole effect of a masterpiece like Pope's *The Rape of the Lock* depends on this strong sense of decorum.

With the development of the movement known as Romanticism,

the attitude towards genre undergoes a change. Wordsworth writes what he calls *Lyrical Ballads*, and he is using the term 'lyrical' not in its ancient sense of something to be sung to an accompaniment (as presumably all the old folk-ballads are) but in the newer sense of expressing feelings, and particularly the feelings of the poet. His title deliberately yokes two genres, the lyric and the ballad, which are in some respects traditionally incompatible: the ballad primarily narrative, concerned with an action, often dramatic in form, and impersonal in attitude; the lyric, generally highly personal, often exclamatory or rhapsodic in style and form, and concerned not with action but with emotion. It is small wonder that the readers and critics of 1798, confronted with a poem like *Simon Lee*, found difficulty seeing what sort of poem it was, and what it was trying to do. It was narrative in that it described a little incident, but the incident seemed wholly trivial, not of the sort found in *Chevy Chase*, in *Lord Randall*, or in *Sir Patrick Spens*. The stanza was a familiar ballad stanza, and the diction was simple and homely, but the stanza did not thrust itself along with the vigorous swing of the real ballad, nor did the diction add to the impetus with the formulas of phrase, repetitions, and refrains of the true ballad. As to the lyrical, what was lyrical about a trivial anecdote of an aged and enfeebled huntsman?

As Wordsworth was to explain later in his preface, what he was doing was to create a new kind of poetry, a new form. His purpose is to deal with primary and universal human feelings, as found in simple people in ordinary situations, and to bring the reader to reflect upon the implications, as he has reflected upon them. The implications are not to be made explicit and elaborated upon by the poet; they are to be discovered by the reader through his own reflections. The poems are to give the reader, not a set of thoughts and emotions, but the seeds of thought and emotion. These are poems to be read actively, not passively. Wordsworth consequently is deliberately avoiding, on the one hand, the kind of stirring action usual in the ballad, and on the other, the kind of passionate eloquence usual in the lyric. Yet, as the title of the volume suggests, he wants to make some use of the traditional ideas associated with the genres of ballad and lyric. The nature of this use is the crucial point of this rather long digression. Wordsworth is looking at genre in a quite different way from that of his eighteenth-century predecessors. He is thinking, not in terms of formal definition, of decorum, of limitations in theme, style, and diction to what is appropriate to that sort of poem, but rather in terms of the kind of associations of ideas acquired historically by a genre. He is working, in a sense, in an opposite way from the traditional. Formal definition of the genre, after all, starts with a general concept of the ideas associated with, say, epic, or tragic, or pastoral, and then seeks rules of form to give perfect expression to the concept. Wordsworth is moving back, away from the formal definition to the general idea and associations. 'Ballad' for him is associated with something like 'folk-song', with the unsophisticated life and emotions of simple people. Part of the conventional form he can use in this association; the stanza is an unsophisticated one, and he can use the simple and 'unpoetic' diction. Other associations he does not want, and must deliberately exclude. The ballad has come to have 'Gothic' associations of spells, and witchcraft, of natural and supernatural horrors. In these, as he says, the 'action gives importance to the feelings'; that is, action is primary, and feelings merely the conventional ones tied to the action. He wants the feelings to give importance to the action, so he chooses actions in themselves unimportant. This approach to the genres as traditional forms, then, is to see them as modes of poetry, embodying sets of associations of ideas, of atmosphere, of moods, of emotional tones, which historically have been developed into poetic forms and structures so that elements of the familiar form will, by association, call up in the reader a complex set of ideas and attitudes. These the poet can use as selectively or as collectively as he wishes.

In this new and freer attitude towards genre, the Romantics generally follow Wordsworth, Tennyson most conspicuously. In his youthful experiments, as we have seen, he practises the styles and tones of a vast variety of genres until he can create a whole set of moods and effects, heroic, elegiac, idyllic, pictorially romantic, satiric, objurgative, simply reflective, pastoral, lushly exotic, and so on. He learns the modes of traditional genres, and invents new stanza forms for other complex effects. He also starts experimenting with the blending or fusion of genres. Some of his experiments are so totally successful, and consequently appear so inevitable, that they are seldom recognized as experiments. His poems on classical subjects, perhaps the most popular and most admired of his works, are all experiments in genre. He takes themes of epic origin, and powerfully associated with Homeric sources, so that they carry with them a strong epic context, and treats them in non-epic modes. *Oenone*, for example, with its epic theme of the judgement of Paris, he approaches obliquely, through Oenone, and casts it primarily into the form of a pastoral elegy with refrain. The opulent style, with its echoes of Theocritus, Ovid, and Milton, and the rich pictorialism of the descriptions, gives way towards the end of the poem to a sterner style, with epic and tragic echoes:

> O mother, hear me yet before I die.
> Hear me, O earth, I will not die alone,
> Lest their shrill happy laughter come to me
> Walking the cold and starless road of Death
> Uncomforted . . .
> All earth and air seem only burning fire.

The 'ornate' style, to which so many critics seem to object on *a priori* grounds, without asking what its function and effect are, here creates a sense of a world of surpassing richness and beauty, brought to destruction by Paris's rash choice. The idyllic world of Oenone is overwhelmed by the iron world of the epic of Troy.

Within this frame, the elegiac lament of Oenone, is set the action of the choice of Paris. As Herè and Pallas successively present their arguments and persuasions to Paris, the focus of attention moves from Oenone to him, and the tone and style of the poem change. The speeches of the two goddesses are majestic enough, but they are not couched in the same sort of ornate style as the earlier lament. And the nature of their inducements changes the whole aspect of the poem. Each is offering Paris, not single and specific rewards, but a whole pattern of life, in each case a life 'likest gods', 'like a God's'. Each, then, is defining the god-like life, and with it the *summum bonum*, the highest good man seeks. Herè offers power, power over others, 'which in all action is the end of all' – namely, that which all men seek. Men 'in power only, are like gods, who have attained Rest in a happy place and quiet seats Above the thunder, with undying bliss In knowledge of their own supremacy'. This is once more the ideal of the secure Epicurean gods, secure, quiet and remote through power.

Pallas offers another kind of power, power over self – this is the 'sovereign power'. The ironic force of the ambiguities of the two words, 'sovereign' and 'power', provides the pivot of the carefully balanced contrast between the two speeches. 'Self-reverence, self-knowledge, self-control, These three alone lead life to sovereign power'. She offers no life of rest and security, but one of 'shocks, dangers, and deeds, until endurance grow Sinewed with action, and the full-grown will, Circled through all experiences, pure law, Commeasure perfect freedom'. For Herè, will is the arbitrary exercise of power over others, law the arbitrary edict of a ruler, freedom the power to be arbitrary. At every point, and through every key word, we are made aware of conflicting philosophies, religious, ethical, and political, upon which a life may be based. Paris is making a choice, not of a suitable winner of the golden apple, but of his own future. He can choose to seek power and ease, wisdom and self-discipline, or, with Aphroditè, mere sensual pleasure. And the poem becomes here something very different from the brilliant pictorial treatment of a favourite scene for painters, or from the rich exploitation of a romantic theme from the classics. Paris becomes Everyman, making the choice of a way of life which each of us must make. When he rejects the life offered by Pallas, which Oenone and Tennyson and the reader recognize as the fitting life for a man who would realize the highest human potential, and chooses the life of sensuality, he chooses, like the hollow man in *The Vision of Sin*, the life that leads to destruction.

The modulation of the theme into the solemn and universal application of the judgement scene is accompanied by a modulation of style, particularly in the speeches of Herè and Pallas. With Paris's decision made, the poet modulates again back to the elegiac lament, but the stern solemnity of the choice carries its tone over, and prepares for the quick change of tone in the lament:

> 'They came, they cut away my tallest pines . . .
> Never, never more
> Shall lone Oenone see the morning mist
> Sweep through them; never see them overlaid
> With narrow moon-lit slips of silver cloud,
> Between the loud stream and the trembling stars.'

This is 'high' style, but not 'ornate' in the way of the earlier passages. The world of rich beauty is destroyed.

The Death of Oenone, written when the poet was eighty, is, as a recent critic has noted with apparent approval, much less ornate in style. Since it is in effect a sequel to or conclusion of *Oenone* it quite naturally moves on from the point at which the first poem ends. The style is essentially the 'high' and serious style into which *Oenone* modulates at the close. It records the deaths of the ruined Paris, 'no longer beauteous as a God', 'Lame, crookèd, reeling, livid, through the mist', struck by a poisoned arrow in the fight at Troy, and of Oenone, who, finally purged of her bitterness at the sight of his body on the funeral pyre, leapt into the flames, 'And mixt herself with *him* and past in fire.' The rich, ornate style of the earlier poem would be as inappropriate to the subject here as it is effective in relation to the subject there.

The other poems on classical epic themes, *The Lotos-Eaters* and *Ulysses*, also exploit the epic context while avoiding the epic form. *Ulysses* makes most direct use of the context, both by allusion and by direct echoes of epic style, but its subtle and ironic development is far removed from the straightforward epic manner and, in fact, as the arguments of critics have shown, leaves a great deal of ambiguity hovering round Ulysses' heroic status. Even its form is ambiguous: at a casual glance it can be taken for a dramatic monologue of a simple sort, but closer examination suggests, as John Pettigrew has shown, that half is soliloquy, half public address.

Even in what seems Tennyson's most traditional poetry, then, he is experimenting with genre, mixing modes, using various styles to create echoes, calling up association through patterns of diction, and modifying the general emotional atmospheres that traditionally belong to each genre. Elsewhere he conducts more radical experiments. In *Maud* he creates a new genre, which he calls monodrama, and in *In Memoriam* he modifies the traditional elegy so extensively as to make it virtually a new form. His largest work, the *Idylls of the King*, also creates a new form of its own, drawing freely on the effects of a number of genres, drama, allegory, epic, romance, and symbolist poetry, to fashion a structure *sui generis* of immense complexity and richness. It would take a number of volumes to explore all these works, and in fact many volumes have already done a good deal of exploration.

In the next chapter we shall consider some aspects of these works of special relevance to this study. But first we must notice some less radical, but very interesting experiments.

The first, *Enoch Arden*, is at a superficial view a fairly simple experiment. It was written in 1861–2 from a story given to Tennyson by his friend Thomas Woolner of a fisherman who signed on as sailor for a long voyage, was shipwrecked and believed lost, returned home long after to find his wife happily re-married, and kept silent about his identity until his death. As Tennyson's contemporaries and later critics have noted, the theme is similar to one of Crabbe's, and might be generally considered as belonging to the genre of domestic tragedy in humble life one associates with Crabbe's verse. But in Tennyson's treatment of the theme, and in his elaboration and expansion of the bare elements of the story, there is no similarity to Crabbe's methods. Crabbe was called by one of his Romantic critics 'a Pope in worsted stockings', a biased but shrewd description. For Crabbe's intentions and methods are essentially eighteenth-century: he intends to 'paint the cot As truth will see it, and as bards will not', to avoid the 'poetic', and to show the life of the simple people of his parish, and especially their tragedies, in a direct and unvarnished style. In this he is at one with neo-classical conceptions of truth and of poetic decorum. What Tennyson does with his treatment is to challenge eighteenth-century preconceptions of decorum. First of all, he refuses to accept the definition of a 'low' subject, for which a 'low' style is fitting. He rejects the notion that the deeds of kings and nobles are 'high' subjects, those of the humble 'low'. He sees the behaviour of Enoch Arden as essentially heroic, and hence fit for 'high' treatment. As a result, the poem has had a peculiar history. From being one of the most popular in the years after its publication in 1864, and popular with a very wide range of readers, from those who translated it into Latin verse to those who read it in cottages or in distant mining camps, it has become now one of his most neglected. It was a main target of attack in Walter Bagehot's famous essay on the ornate and grotesque styles in poetry, and few have since stopped to ask whether Bagehot could have been wrong. The growing unpopularity of the high style, and insensitivity to it, reflected in the preference now shown for prosaic prose translations of Homer and Virgil over the translations by Pope and Dryden, has led to a general prejudice against high style in any context, let alone a low one. As a result, critics follow Bagehot, without perhaps recognizing that Bagehot is himself a throw-back to the narrowest sort of eighteenth-century criticism. Instead of continuing the experimental approach to genre and style of the Romantics, Bagehot goes back to the fixed definitions. His famous jeer at Tennyson's description of Enoch's catch of fish as 'ocean-spoil In ocean-smelling osier' should fall flat with critics who admire the author of *Beowulf* for describing the sea as the whale-road, or a ship as a foamy-necked floater.

The unhappy effect of an essay like Bagehot's is that it induces in the critic a nervous self-consciousness, so that he reads, convinced that he ought to be repelled by the ornate style, shuddering wherever he finds it, and in his anxiety finding it everywhere. The unsophisticated and unselfconscious reader of Tennyson's own generation, happily ignorant of these subtleties, was moved by the story, by the accuracy of Tennyson's psychological insight, by the vividness of the descriptions, and by a sense that the story was being told in a style which perhaps at times seemed to him as dignified and grand as that of the Bible or the Prayer Book, and which enhanced the dignity and nobility of the action and characters. What the modern and sophisticated reader can do is to accept the style without prejudice, as a poetic idiom linked, not to a particular kind of subject-matter, let alone subject-matter attached to particular social levels or occupations, but to certain tones and associations loosely known as 'heroic'. He can also take a closer look at the actual style of the narrative to see in fact how much there is of the ornate in Bagehot's sense. If he does this last, what will he find?

He will find how rare in the 911 lines of the poem the 'ornate' is. In the first third of the poem, he will read that Enoch 'Thrice had plucked a life From the dread sweep of the down-streaming sea' (ll. 54–5), that Annie's first-born was 'the rosy idol of her solitudes' (l. 90), that Enoch gathered 'ocean-spoil In ocean-smelling osier' (ll. 98), and that Enoch sold fish to the Hall, 'Whose Friday fare was Enoch's ministering' (l. 100). Annie's marriage is when 'Enoch's golden ring had girt Her finger' (ll. 157–8). He will find a few 'poetic' similes:

> So now that shadow of mischance appeared
> No graver than as when some little cloud
> Cuts off the fiery highway of the sun,
> And isles a light in the offing. . . . (ll. 128–31)

and others at ll. 206–9 and 363–4. He will find an occasional, but rare, Miltonic inversion, as at l. 201, 'Him running on thus hopefully she heard', and at ll. 363–4, 'Him, like the working bee in blossom-dust, Blanched with his mill, they found'. In short, he will find in the first three hundred lines or so about a dozen examples, four of which appear within a ten-line boundary. Bagehot has chosen, not a typical, but a most unusual passage. In the rest of the poem, Bagehot's sort of ornate is even rarer. Tennyson himself speaks of 'the simplicity of the narrative', and the overwhelming proportion of the narrative, the predominant texture of the style, is simple and direct. The passage immediately following the one made famous by Bagehot is a genuinely typical one:

> Then came a change, as all things human change.
> Ten miles to northward of the narrow port
> Opened a larger haven: Thither used
> Enoch at times to go by land or sea;
> And once when there, and clambering on a mast
> In harbour, by mischance he slipt and fell:
> A limb was broken when they lifted him;
> And while he lay recovering there, his wife
> Bore him another son, a sickly one . . . .

Or take, for another example, the swift and sparse description of the wreck:

> Less lucky her home-voyage: at first indeed
> Through many a fair sea-circle, day by day,
> Scarce rocking, her full-busted figure-head
> Stared o'er the ripple feathering from her bows:
> Then followed calms, and then winds variable,
> Then baffling, a long course of them; and last
> Storm, such as drove her under moonless heavens
> Till hard upon the cry of 'breakers' came
> The crash of ruin, and the loss of all
> But Enoch and two others. Half the night,
> Buoyed upon floating tackle and broken spars,
> These drifted, stranding on an isle at morn,
> Rich, but the loneliest in a lonely sea.

The many passages of conversation throughout the poem are also vivid in their direct simplicity.

What Bagehot and those who follow him fail to realize is that Tennyson does not identify a high or elevated style with an ornate style, as this poem, as well as dozens of others of his, will demonstrate. In this poem as in many of his mature poems, Tennyson is influenced by Wordsworth – or, to put it in another way, is using techniques learned from Wordsworth. And one of the notable things about Wordsworth's technique is his command of a variety of elevated styles, and the rather complex way in which he uses ornate diction. One of the best examples is the familiar 'Nutting' episode included in the *Prelude*. Here Wordsworth describes the ragged-looking little expedition of children setting out to gather hazel nuts in terms of brilliantly accoutred knights starting on a romantic quest. Superficially, the style suggests only the comedy of the mock-heroic, the application of inappropriately high style to a low subject. But Wordsworth gives the style a double function, so that we see the expedition from the child's point of view, filled with the sense of high adventure, romance, and excitement, and also from the adult's, tinged with the comedy of a little group of urchins setting out with such high hearts to plunder the woods. The ornate style here is used with a rich and complex ambivalence, in which the serious and the tongue-in-cheek are fused. So it seems to be in *Enoch Arden*, in its rare appearances there. Its most conspicuous use is in the passage describing the seven golden years of Enoch's marriage, when all was romance and adventure to him – even catching and selling fish. It may not be accident that Tennyson's poem also contains a nutting incident, reminiscent of Wordsworth's:

> So Philip rested with her well-content;
> While all the younger ones with jubilant cries
> Broke from their elders, and tumultuously
> Down through the whitening hazels made a plunge
> To the bottom, and dispersed, and bent or broke
> The lithe reluctant boughs to tear away
> Their tawny clusters, crying to each other
> And calling, here and there, about the wood.

The symbolic overtones of this little scene in Tennyson's poem are very similar to that in Wordsworth's.

It is obviously not on the ornate that Tennyson relies for elevation of the style of the heroic. He relies mainly on the power of the simple and direct, with touches of heightening provided by occasional biblical turns of phrase, by the sparing use of epic inversions of syntax:

> Thus over Enoch's early silvering head
> The sunny and rainy seasons came and went
> Year after year. His hopes to see his own,
> And pace the sacred old familiar fields,
> Not yet had perished, . . .
>
> And dull the voyage was with long delays,
> The vessel scarce sea-worthy; but evermore
> His fancy fled before the lazy wind
> Returning . . . .

Note particularly the force of the description of Enoch's walk to his old house:

> On the nigh-naked tree the robin piped
> Disconsolate, and through the dripping haze
> The dead weight of the dead leaf bore it down:
> Thicker the drizzle grew, deeper the gloom;
> Last, as it seemed, a great mist-blotted light
> Flared on him, and he came upon the place.
>   Then down the long street having slowly stolen,
> His heart foreshadowing all calamity,
> His eyes upon the stones, he reached the house
> Where Annie lived and loved him . . . .

The diction is simple, not ornate; the effect is created through syntactical movement, tonality, and tempo, and of course through the symbolism of the images. The slow movement of the descriptive lines breaks into movement with 'Flared on him', and then 'he came upon the place', with its ultimate simplicity of statement, biblical in tone, brings all to a pause, to be followed by the inverted and lengthened line, still made up of bare and simple words, but poetic in its syntax and tonalities, describing his half-reluctant, fearful movement towards the house itself.

The predominant style of the poem, what might be called the stylistic warp of its poetic texture, is this, the elevated simple, not the ornate. Variations, which might be thought of as the woof, naturally follow the design of the structure. The poem is roughly symmetrical, the first quarter, to line 243, narrating the events from childhood of the three main characters up to Enoch's departure; the second quarter, to line 522, narrating events at home during Enoch's ten years of absence, ending with Annie's marriage to Philip and the birth of their child; the third quarter, to line 662, describing Enoch's voyages, wreck, marooning, life on the island, eventual rescue and return; the final quarter, to line 911, Enoch's sacrifice, death and funeral. Part one, Enoch, Annie, and Philip; part two, Annie and Philip; part three, Enoch; part four, Philip, Annie, and Enoch – this is the symmetry. The first part calls for a movement from the idyllic and pastoral to the near tragic as Enoch's fortunes decline; part two for movement from tragic back to something close to the idyllic again; part three for the development of the irony of a setting conventionally idyllic and primitively beautiful, an earthly Paradise which becomes a Hell; part four for ironic contrast of the happy domesticity of Philip and Annie and the heroic suffering and endurance of Enoch.

These movements, with their powerful dramatic effects, are accomplished with great economy. A single paragraph in part three creates the whole effect, a paragraph of rich imagery, twenty-seven lines long and organized into a single powerful sentence:

> The mountain wooded to the peaks, the lawns
> And winding glades high up like ways to Heaven,
> The slender coco's dropping crown of plumes,
> The lightning flash of insect and of bird,
> The lustre of the long convolvuluses
> That coiled around the stately stems, and ran
> Even to the limit of the land, the glows
> And glories of the broad belt of the world,
> All these he saw; but what he fain had seen
> He could not see, the kindly human face,
> Nor ever hear a kindly voice, but heard
> The myriad shriek of wheeling ocean-fowl,
> The league-long roller thundering on the reef,
> The moving whisper of huge trees that branched
> And blossomed in the zenith, or the sweep
> Of some precipitous rivulet to the wave,
> As down the shore he ranged, or all day long
> Sat often in the seaward-gazing gorge,
> A shipwrecked sailor, waiting for a sail:
> No sail from day to day, but every day
> The sunrise broken into scarlet shafts
> Among the palms and ferns and precipices;
> The blaze upon the waters to the east;
> The blaze upon his island overhead;
> The blaze upon the waters to the west;
> Then the great stars that globed themselves in Heaven,
> The hollower-bellowing ocean, and again
> The scarlet shafts of sunrise – but no sail.

The passage opens with a scene of rich, varied, and timeless beauty, full of suggestions of the idyllic and paradisal – 'ways to Heaven', 'crown of plumes', 'lustre', 'stately', 'glows and glories'. It then modulates to a contrast between nature, indifferent or hostile, and the 'kindly' human, the double suggestion of 'kindly' as 'belonging to one's kind' emphasized by repetition; sight is largely replaced by sound as he listens for a human voice and hears only 'the myriad shriek', the 'thundering', the 'whisper' or the 'sweep' of the rivulet; as the passage ends, the whole landscape is reduced to a pitiless clock monotonously measuring off time without change: the sun rises, blazes to the east, blazes overhead, blazes to the west, sinks, and rises again. And all its meaning to the lonely marooned sailor is summed up in the final '– but no sail'.

This scene is deftly contrasted in the next few lines with another landscape, which becomes the infinitely nostalgic and romantic one, set against the conventionally romantic and exotic island paradise:

> . . . the chill
> November dawns and dewy-glooming downs,
> The gentle shower, the smell of dying leaves,
> And the low moan of leaden-coloured seas.

Nothing could bring out more powerfully the horror, in Enoch's situation, of one of those 'summer-isles of Eden lying in dark purple spheres of sea', of the steady blaze of sun, the blaze of colour, the ceaseless growth of the tropics. And nothing, in a sense, could emphasize more strongly the central intention of the poem, for this passage presents a Romantic illusion and destroys it, presents one of the ornate commonplaces of Romantic primitivism and shows its falseness.

The other dramatic contrast is also simply established in the picture of Philip's home as the returned Enoch secretly looks into it:

> For cups and silver on the burnished board
> Sparkled and shone; so genial was the hearth . . .
> Now when the dead man come to life beheld
> His wife his wife no more, and saw the babe
> Hers, yet not his, upon the father's knee,
> And all the warmth, the peace, the happiness, . . .
> Then he . . .

Staggered and shook, holding the branch, and feared
To send abroad a shrill and terrible cry,
Which in one moment, like the blast of doom,
Would shatter all the happiness of the hearth.

The one word in the passage which might be considered ornate
is 'genial', used here in the classical (and Miltonic) sense. Combined
with the repeated word 'hearth', itself simple but powerful in
association, it suggests a household blessed by the gods, a holy
place, just as the cups and silver shining on the board suggest not
only comfort and prosperity but the sacramental. Enoch, outside
in the night, looking in on this little holy Paradise, this blessed
family, as Satan in *Paradise Lost* looked down at that other
Paradise, has no temptation to destroy it, but fearing only his own
weakness, prays for the strength not to break in upon their peace.
This is the moment of his highest heroism, which is throughout a
religious heroism, and Tennyson's description of the family scene
not only brings out the intense emotion of Enoch's trial, but also,
in emphasizing the scene not simply as domestic but holy, makes
clear the nature and motives of his sacrifice. The economy and
simplicity of his method are again notable.

The conclusion of the poem has often been criticized:

So past the strong heroic soul away.
And when they buried him the little port
Had seldom seen a costlier funeral.

Most of the attackers point out the obvious, which they seem to
think Tennyson must have missed: that the costly funeral did
Enoch no good. Since Tennyson's poetry is constantly exploiting
ironies, it is strange that critics should not be aware that it is doing
so here, and that he inserts the word 'costlier', which he could
easily have avoided, quite deliberately. It is of course ironic that
the money spent on his funeral could, in his youth, have saved
him from his whole tragedy, just as it is ironic that his wife can
enjoy the comforts, and his children the education, he sought for
them only by his presumed death. He could not, living, have
accepted these from Philip without destroying his own strong
dignity, and independence. Finally, there is an irony in all
funerals; in a sense they are all futile gestures. It makes no
difference to the dead man, to be sure, whether he is hastily
shovelled into a hole in the ground with a prayer or is given a

state funeral. But it is naïve to think that a funeral is simply for the benefit of the dead. It is a public ceremony, with the usual complex purposes of public ceremonies. One purpose is to honour publicly some achievement of the dead man, or some quality in him or in his life, that the community values, and to reaffirm the value. The little community in which Enoch died, and particularly his wife, Annie, and his true friend, Philip, had no chance to do anything for Enoch while he lived; all they can do now is honour him by giving him a hero's funeral. They too know how inadequate this is; the alternative is not to do him this honour, not to praise him and his sacrifice by this public ceremony. To object to it is to set too high a value on money, to think it should not be wasted on a celebration of true heroism and piety. Simple folk think differently, and this is a tale of simple folk. Tennyson was quite right in insisting that this ending is 'quite necessary to the perfection of the Poem and the simplicity of the narrative'.

The Princess is perhaps unique among Tennyson's works in that its form is largely influenced by his didactic purpose. Elsewhere the experiments and innovations which characterize his poetic practice, the novel stanza forms, the unorthodox verse-lengths, the deliberate use of unexpected genre, or the mixture of genres, can be explained on purely aesthetic grounds, as attempts to widen the range of effects in English poetry. In *The Princess*, however, the aesthetic problem is a consequence of, or is at least inseparable from, the problem of his didactic strategy. The subject with which the poem deals, the rights of women, and the place of women in society, was one which seemed to foster 'the falsehood of extremes'. To many men, the struggle for female emancipation was purely and simply comic: to many women, deeply and fiercely tragic. Both extremes, of facetiousness and of earnestness, made for tightly shut minds. As Tennyson knew, a comic treatment would delight the men, infuriate the women, and confirm both sets of prejudice; a solemn one would please the women and disgust the men. His difficult task is to persuade both sides, to write something which both sides will read and which will moderate both extremes. This task obviously confronts him with a very difficult aesthetic problem.

In *The Rape of the Lock* Pope had faced a not dissimilar situation on a minor scale, but it was relatively easy for him to sacrifice the didactic purpose of healing the breach between Lord Petre and the Fermors to the aesthetic purpose of the pure genre, and the serious implications of the Cave of Spleen and the direct di-dacticism of Clarissa's speech are kept rigorously subordinate and even subservient to the single mock-heroic tenor of the poem. The importance Tennyson attaches to the subject he is treating, and the much greater freedom he always shows in his approach to genre, make a treatment like Pope's an unlikely one for Tennyson, but the parallel, imperfect as it is, throws some light on Tennyson's procedure.

At the outset, he frees himself from the demands of any recognized formal genre by the device of the multiple narration; the poem has arisen from a game of impromptu storytelling by seven narrators who contribute successive parts. The conversation among these narrators before the storytelling begins, and the description of their surroundings, prepare for a 'medley' with a miscellany of subject-matter and tones. The device also frees the poet conventionally from responsibility for the substance of the story, although it is announced at the end that he was 'to bind the scatter'd scheme of seven together in one sheaf' and, most important of all, to choose the style.

> What style could suit?
> The men required that I should give throughout
> The sort of mock heroic gigantesque, ...
> The women ... hated banter ....
>   Why
> Not make her true-heroic – true-sublime,
> ... And I, betwixt them both, to please them both,
> And yet to give the story as it rose,
> I moved as in a strange diagonal,
> And maybe neither pleased myself nor them.

The image of the diagonal is a happy one: it suggests accurately the sense of linear continuity by which the poem moves – no poem gives actually less effect of chance or of haphazard direction – and at the same time suggests also an ironic ambiguity, since a diagonal may be thought of either as a straight line from one corner to its opposite, or as a line which retains a fixed distance from two sides perpendicular to each other. Tennyson's diagonal does not simply run from mock-heroic to heroic, from ridiculous to sublime; it operates in a delicate balance from the start.

It is indeed necessary to his purpose to avoid establishing an unequivocal tone at the beginning; he needs an unequivocally serious tone at the end, but not an unequivocally frivolous one at the first. And one has only to recall an example of the strict mock-heroic to realize within what limits Tennyson has confined the burlesque. In *The Princess*, one looks in vain for the usual sequence of mock-epic conventions; there are no invocations, no epic catalogues, no supernatural machinery, no epic games.

The poem opens, indeed, with no suggestion of the mock-epic; the genre established with the first lines is that of romance, or of fairy-tale, rather than epic, and the style carries no suggestion of either epic or mock-epic:

> A prince I was, blue-eyed, and fair in face,
> Of temper amorous, as the first of May,
> With lengths of yellow ringlet, like a girl,
> For on my cradle shone the Northern star.
> There lived an ancient legend in our house ...

The first-person narration, the conversational tone, the informal syntax, are as remote from epic style as the matter is remote from epic matter. The effect produced is, in a sense, neutral; neither serious nor comic, neither elevated nor low. The Prince goes on to speak of the 'ancient legend' that

> Some sorcerer, whom a far-off grandsire burnt
> Because he cast no shadow, had foretold,
> Dying, that none of all our blood should know
> The shadow from the substance, and that one
> Should come to fight with shadows and to fall ...

This establishes at the outset the theme of ambiguity, of shadow and substance, repeated from time to time throughout the poem. Each time this theme is introduced, it is brought in abruptly, so as to break the established mood and tone; it is made to interrupt a sharply focused scene and suddenly dissolve it, so that the reader, like the Prince, is momentarily caught up in uncertainty. It is only at the end of the poem, when the tone is to be clear and unequivocal, that the theme of ambiguity is resolved, and the Prince's 'haunting sense of hollow shows' leaves him. I am concerned here, not with the meaning of the Prince's seizures, but with the effect of the passages describing them; with their function as interruptions to prevent an atmosphere from becoming too firmly established, and with their function as signposts to ambivalence.

As to Ida herself, in this opening section we are strongly influenced by the Prince's view of her:

> Still I wore her picture by my heart,
> And one dark tress; and all around them both
> Sweet thoughts would swarm as bees about their queen.
> ... I rose and past
> Thro' the wild woods that hung about the town;
> Found a still place, and pluck'd her likeness out;
> Laid it on flowers, and watch'd it lying bathed
> In the green gleam of dewy-tassell'd trees ...
> Proud look'd the lips: but while I meditated
> A wind arose and rush'd upon the South,
> And shook the songs, the whispers, and the shrieks
> Of the wild woods together; and a Voice
> Went with it, 'Follow, follow, thou shalt win.'

Humour is introduced very sparingly in the opening section, and never is allowed to touch Ida herself. The first light touches of the comic are applied to the two kings, fathers of the Prince and Princess. The Prince's father, inflamed with wrath by the letter announcing that Ida refuses to marry his son, tore the letter, 'snow'd it down', 'then he chew'd the thrice-turn'd cud of wrath, and cook'd his spleen.' Ida's father, King Gama ('a little dry old man', 'airing a snowy hand and signet gem',) vaguely remembers that there had been a compact, 'a kind of ceremony – I think the year in which our olives fail'd'. There is nothing in the presentation of the two kings to lend them dignity; Gama's account of his difficulties with Ida simply reinforces the impression of his own ineffectualness.

As the Prince writes seeking admission for himself and his friends, disguised as girls, to Ida's college, the touch of comedy in the description of his assumed lady-like back-hand script, 'such a hand as when a field of corn Bows all its ears before the roaring East,' follows a first description of Ida's college in which nothing of the comic is suggested, and which is rapidly modulated to a serious close:

> We gain'd
> A little street half garden and half house;
> But scarce could hear each other speak for noise
> Of clocks and chimes, like silver hammers falling

> On silver anvils, and the splash and stir
> Of fountains spouted up and showering down
> In meshes of the jasmine and the rose:
> And all about us peal'd the nightingale,
> Rapt in her song, and careless of the snare . . . .
> And then to bed, where half in doze I seem'd
> To float about a glimmering night, and watch
> A full sea glazed with muffled moonlight, swell
> On some dark shore just seen that it was rich.

This solemn coda to part one is, it will be recognized, in a different style from the fairy-tale opening, as well as from the comic passages. In its diction and in its rhythm, and in the solemnity of its mood, it prepares for the first of the lyrics, 'As through the land at eve we went.'

The dominant effect of the opening of the narrative is undoubtedly serious, in a rich vein of lyricism; the seriousness is continued into the first description of the college and of Ida herself. The style is here heightened to suggest the true heroic:

> Out we paced,
> I first, and following thro' the porch that sang
> All round with laurel, issued in a court
> Compact of lucid marbles, boss'd with lengths
> Of classic frieze . . .
> There at a board by tome and paper sat,
> With two tame leopards couch'd beside her throne,
> All beauty compass'd in a female form,
> The Princess; liker to the inhabitant
> Of some clear planet close upon the Sun,
> Than our man's earth; such eyes were in her head,
> And so much grace and power, breathing down
> From over her arch'd brows, with every turn
> Lived thro' her to the tips of her long hands . . .

This is as solemnly ornate as the descriptions in *Oenone*, and creates, especially as prepared for by the passages in part one, so dignified and lofty an impression of the Princess that nothing she says or does can seem to us merely comic. And the style of these passages, though elevated enough to suggest the heroic, is kept direct and restrained, almost entirely free of mannerism; and consequently entirely remote from the mock-heroic or burlesque.

By the beginning of the second part of the poem, then, we have been induced to think of Ida in poetic and dignified terms. As a result, when the comic is allowed to play on her, it can never reduce her to the ridiculous. At worst, her essential nobility can be seen to be touched here and there by folly; more properly, she can be seen as in the partial grasp of a noble wrong-headedness, a magnanimous eccentricity. The comic spirit can illuminate her defects of judgement, but not impugn her grandeur and rightness of intention.

We recognize the application of this principle in her first speeches. In her little speech of welcome to the disguised Prince and his friends, she first rebukes Cyril for using 'the tinsel clink of compliment', but goes on to a statement of her aims, which the narrator describes, with no necessary suspicion of irony, as 'those high words'. And in her parting advice, although it begins with the at least half comic: 'Ye are green wood, see ye warp not', and although her description of the college statues brings a comic reminder of how exclusively masculine is the history of the heroic as normally taught, she ends with a perfectly serious, and in the context moving injunction: 'Better not be at all than not be noble.'

The same method can be seen in her presidential address to the students. It starts by exploiting the comic effect of condensation and of translation of direct into indirect speech. This is, of course, one of Dickens's common devices, especially as applied to oratory. Ida's speech makes a rapid historical survey of the place of woman in society, starting with her favourite piece of science, the nebular hypothesis, and moving rapidly through evolution:

> ... The planets: then the monster, then the man;
>   Tattoo'd or woaded, winter-clad in skins,
>   Raw from the prime, and crushing down his mate ...
>   Thereupon she took
>   A bird's-eye-view of all the ungracious past;
>   Glanced at the legendary Amazon
>   As emblematic of a nobler age;
>   Appraised the Lycian custom ...
>   Ran down the Persian, Grecian, Roman lines
>   Of empire, and the woman's state in each,
>   How far from just; till warming with her theme
>   She fulmined out her scorn of laws Salique
>   And little-footed China, touch'd on Mahomet
>   With much contempt, and came to chivalry:

When some respect, however slight, was paid
To woman . . .
However then commenced the dawn: a beam
Had slanted forward, falling in a land
Of promise; fruit would follow.

The passage manages to combine suggestions of a tub-thumping party speech, a lecture in a survey course, and a reporter's mangled account of a public address. Those who have had public lectures reported will particularly wonder whether the splendid mixture of metaphors at the end is really Ida's or the reporter's. But there is no doubt that so far the speech is presented in comic terms, just though Ida's sentiments might be. But from this point on, the reporting of the speech changes its mode; it becomes less compressed, the ideas are given more elaboration, and are presented without the implicitly derogatory 'glanced at', 'appraised', 'ran down', 'fulmined'. The presentation moves towards direct speech, and a direct and more persuasive style. As a result, when we come to the conclusion we are ready for actual direct speech, and ready also to take with a minimum of irony the introduction to these last words: 'She rose upon a wind of prophecy Dilating on the future.' And the quality of her last words enforces not only our agreement but again our respect for Ida:

> Everywhere
> Two heads in council, two beside the hearth,
> Two in the tangled business of the world,
> Two in the liberal offices of life,
> Two plummets dropt for one to sound the abyss
> Of science, and the secrets of the mind:
> Musician, painter, sculptor, critic, more:
> And everywhere the broad and bounteous Earth
> Should bear a double growth of those rare souls,
> Poets, whose thoughts enrich the blood of the world.

In each of the speeches the technique is the same, each moves towards an ending in which the serious sincerity of Ida's words is matched by the directness and simplicity of the style. We are returned always to the noble conception of Ida.

A great part of the comedy centres, of course, not directly about Ida but about the women's college, her scheme. Nearly all this comedy is double-edged, since it depends upon the simple

situation of women aping men. It is not long before the question
arises in the reader's mind whether a college which excludes every
male creature is intrinsically any more ridiculous than one which
excludes every female, and whether an education of fact-cramming
or of superficial surveys is any more ridiculous for women than
for men, and whether history from an exclusively feminine
perspective is any more one-sided than from a masculine one. In
so far as Ida'a college is ridiculous, it may be because it imitates a
ridiculous model. This is suggested by the Prince after half a day
of attendance at lectures:

> We dipt in all
> That treats of whatsoever is, the state,
> The total chronicles of man, the mind,
> The morals, something of the frame, the rock,
> The star, the bird, the fish, the shell, the flower,
> Electric, chemic laws, and all the rest,
> And whatsoever can be taught and known;
> Till like three horses that have broken fence,
> And glutted all night long breast-deep in corn,
> We issued gorged with knowledge, and I spoke:
> 'Why, Sirs, they do all this as well as we.'

And again, as part two comes to an end, the comic modulates into
the serious, first by the gentle idyllic description of the college
gardens and finally of the night chapel, where

> the great organ almost burst his pipes,
> Groaning for power, and rolling thro' the court
> A long melodious thunder to the sound
> Of solemn psalms, and silver litanies,
> The work of Ida, to call down from Heaven
> A blessing on her labours for the world.

The day ends with a view of Ida as poet and priestess, holy and
serious of purpose.

The lyric 'Sweet and low' modulates from this solemn close to
the high style of the description of morning which opens part
three:

> Morn in the white wake of the morning star
> Came furrowing all the orient into gold.

There is hardly a note of comedy in this section, unless the reader
is to be amused by feminine interest in geology, 'chattering stony

names / Of shale and hornblende, rag and trap and tuff, / Amygdaloid and trachyte'. The dominant tone is set by two passages. In the first the Prince comments on Ida:

> 'The crane,' I said, 'may chatter of the crane,
> The dove may murmur of the dove, but I
> An eagle clang an eagle to the sphere,
> My princess, O my princess! true she errs,
> But in her own grand way: being herself
> Three times more noble than three score of men,
> She sees herself in every woman else,
> And so she wears her error like a crown
> To blind the truth and me ... whene'er she moves
> The Samian Herè rises and she speaks
> A Memnon smitten with the morning Sun ...'

In the second, Ida answers the Prince's question about evolution in a serious speech which undoubtedly represents Tennyson's own thoughts. She and the Prince have been looking at the fossil bones 'of some vast bulk that lived and roar'd / Before man was'.

> She gazed awhile, and said,
> 'As these rude bones to us, are we to her
> That will be.'

To which the Prince responds with the question: 'Dare we dream of that ... Which wrought us, as the workman and his work, that practice betters?' And she replies:

> 'Let there be light and there was light: 'tis so;
> For was, and is, and will be, are but is;
> And all creation is one act at once,
> The birth of light: but we that are not all,
> As parts, can see but parts, now this, now that,
> And live, perforce, from thought to thought, and make
> One act a phantom of succession: thus
> Our weakness somehow shapes the shadow, Time;
> But in the shadow will we work, and mould
> The woman to the fuller day.'

And this part closes with one of Tennyson's favourite and majestic symbols:

> The Sun
> Grew broader towards his death and fell, and all
> The rosy heights came out above the lawns.

The first three sections of *The Princess*, then, contain little of the comic, and in style move mainly from the lyrically ornate style of romance to the direct rhetoric and simple diction of a true elevated style, with suggestions of the heroic in the Prince's description of Ida. The 'strange Poet-princess with her grand imagination' has been firmly established in a fitting stylistic context.

In the fourth part, the central one of the poem, the comic is allowed fuller scope, in a formula indicated by the Prince's words at the end of the section:

> The Princess with her monstrous woman-guard,
> The jest and earnest working side by side.

Thus the beautiful sunset lyric, 'The splendour falls on castle walls', is followed at once by Ida's 'There sinks the nebulous star we call the Sun, If that hypothesis of theirs be sound'; and the haunting 'Tears, idle tears' is described by Ida as 'moans about the retrospect'. 'O, Swallow, Swallow, flying, flying South' she dismisses as 'a mere love-poem' which minds us of the time 'when we made bricks in Egypt'. If for a Poet-princess she here reveals an unexpectedly comic insensitivity to the lyrical, and an almost Philistine prosiness, we are soon made aware that she recognizes the beauty of the songs, but is (like many another critic) disturbed by the tendency of their themes:

> Thine are fancies hatch'd
> In silken-folded idleness; nor is it
> Wiser to weep a true occasion lost . . .
> But great is song
> Used to great ends: ourself have often tried
> Valkyrian hymns, or into rhythms have dash'd
> The passion of the prophetess; for song
> Is duer unto freedom, force and growth
> Of spirit than to junketing and love.

She is of sufficiently Wagnerian stature to make the notion of her Valkyrian hymns plausible rather than comic. The allusions also, of course, prepare us for her later fury and inflexibility. There is at the same time a serious side to these passages. As we have noted, the Prince describes Ida repeatedly in terms both of lyrical romance and of the heroic. She herself denies and tries to suppress the lyrical and romantic side of her nature, regarding it as weakness. The vigour of her expressions of contempt for the songs illuminates the vigour of her repression, and indirectly the power of the attraction she feels the songs exerting, and thus the hidden power of the lyrical in her. The Prince's assessment of her character is accurate.

The discovery of the disguised men, and their pursuit by the female proctors, move the tone towards the broad comedy of farce, and here for the first time mock-heroic style plays a considerable part in the pattern. But it is noticeable that there are no sustained passages of mock-heroic, and the mock-heroic is not applied to Ida herself. The images of the Princess that strike on our mind are serious heroic: she is 'all the hopes of half the world'; her wrath is described in a true epic simile which suggests its justice:

> Over brow
> And cheek and bosom brake the wrathful bloom
> As of some fire against a stormy cloud,
> When the wild peasant rights himself, the rick
> Flames, and his anger reddens in the heavens . . .

Two other epic descriptions are applied to her some lines later:

> Not peace she look'd, the Head: but rising up
> Robed in the long night of her deep hair, so
> To the open window moved, remaining there
> Fixt like a beacon-tower above the waves
> Of tempest, when the crimson-rolling eye
> Glares ruin, and the wild birds on the light
> Dash themselves dead. She stretch'd her arms and call'd
> Across the tumult and the tumult fell.

And

> She, ending, waved her hands
> . . . then with a smile, that look'd
> A stroke of cruel sunshine on the cliff,
> When all the glens are drown'd in azure gloom
> Of thunder-shower, she floated to us . . .

Further, the Prince's speech to her is still in the lyrical style of romance, and continues the tone of part one:

> When a boy, you stoop'd to me
> From all high places, lived in all fair lights,
> Came in long breezes rapt from inmost south
> And blown to inmost north; at eve and dawn
> With Ida, Ida, Ida rang the woods;
> The leader wildswan in among the stars
> Would clang it, and lapt in wreaths of glowworm light
> The mellow breaker murmur'd Ida.

Part five of the poem is introduced by the lyric of battle, 'Thy voice is heard thro' rolling drums', and by a brief interlude which returns us to the characters of the prelude, and which is designed to prepare us for a more completely serious treatment. And perhaps nothing could remind us more forcibly than part five that *The Princess* is not primarily mock-heroic. The battle here is not a parody of epic combat, but a serious battle over a serious issue, fought with real weapons and resulting in real wounds. The only elements indeed that might be considered comic here are the utterances of the two royal fathers:

> Look you, Sir!
> Man is the hunter; woman is his game:
> The sleek and shining creatures of the chase.
> We hunt them for the beauty of their skins;
> They love us for it, and we ride them down.

And

> Man for the field and woman for the hearth;
> Man for the sword and for the needle she;
> Man with the head and woman with the heart:
> Man to command and woman to obey;
> All else confusion.

But these crude expressions of male superiority, set in the context of preparation for war, and the determination to crush women by force, have a sardonic and grim effect far from the simply comic. The dominant tone begins to move towards the tragic; the pattern of action becomes indeed tragic in the strict sense. Ida is placed under an almost intolerable burden of gratitude to the Prince: 'He saved my life: my brother slew him for it', yet her pride, after her defeat, makes surrender a very bitter sacrifice. The conflict in her spirit between love and hurt pride, between her sense of obligation and what she still sees as her duty, occupies the rest of the poem, and is intensely serious and moving. The tone and theme are both suggested by the invocation to her:

> O fair and strong and terrible! ...
> But Love and Nature, these are two more terrible
> And stronger.

Elements of true epic style, and in particular the epic comparisons applied to Ida, become more frequent and more extensive, until they reach a climax at the moment of her greatest anguish:

> Seldom she spoke: but oft
> Clomb to the roofs, and gazed alone for hours
> On that disastrous leaguer ... void was her use,
> And she as one that climbs a peak to gaze
> O'er land and main, and sees a great black cloud
> Drag inward from the deeps, a wall of night,
> Blot out the slope of sea from verge to shore,
> And suck the blinding splendour from the sand,
> And quenching lake by lake and tarn by tarn
> Expunge the world: so fared she gazing there ...

This increasing note of the heroic is accompanied by a steady increase in the depth and complexity of the lyrics, culminating in the great Jungfrau song 'Come down, O maid'. At the same time, the lyrics become not only more serious and more complex, but more closely involved in the action, so that the heroic and the lyric become fused.

Tennyson's 'strange diagonal', the line of tone and style through which he makes his poem move, is certainly not a two-dimensional one between a single pair of perpendiculars; it is indeed a strange diagonal, moving through a complex of dimensions, but, like a true diagonal, moving surely and directly to an appointed terminus.

Another very interesting structure is the narrative *Aylmer's Field*, published in 1864. Tennyson worked at it for eighteen months, and found the story, he said, 'incalculably difficult' to tell. 'He often pointed out how hard he had found such and such a passage, how much work and thought it had cost him ...' 'The dry facts' of the story, he said, were 'so prosaic in themselves'. The 'dry facts' were sent to Tennyson by his friend, Thomas Woolner (who also sent him the story of *Enoch Arden*) as a possible subject for a poem. The facts are certainly not 'dry' in the sense of not obviously containing the material for a narrative. They tell of a rich and powerful squire, proud descendant of an ancient family, who has an only daughter. The incumbent of the parish, whose equally ancient family have held the living for generations, has a younger brother. He and the squire's daughter fall in love, the squire learns of it, forbids all association, and starts negotiating a 'suitable' marriage for his daughter, one that will preserve the ancient family and also augment its power and property. She rejects all suitors, is subjected to brutal pressure, goes into a decline, and dies of a fever. The vicar's young brother, at the news of her death, goes mad and commits suicide. The vicar, asked to preach at the girl's funeral on the text (suggested by her mother) 'Behold, your house is left unto you desolate!' – a text which applies to himself as well as to the squire – makes his sermon a denunciation of pride and of the worship of Mammon, and a vehicle for his own grief and sense of outrage at the death of his brother and of his love. The squire and his lady never recover from the death of their daughter and of all their hopes, and, shattered by the realization of their responsibility, themselves go into a decline. After their deaths the great Hall is torn down. These are the facts, presented here in as dry a form as possible.

The problem Tennyson faced was primarily one of genre. The facts themselves are clearly capable of more than one sort of development. They contain more than one sort of tragedy, for example. Seen from a focus held steadily on the squire (Tennyson's Sir Aylmer Aylmer), his plans for the continuance of his ancient family and power, his schemes 'for his daughter's good' and their frustration in total catastrophe, the story is a tragedy both in the ancient sense – a man of great position led by *hubris* to a decision which brings about his own destruction – and also in the medieval sense – the fall of a great man. If attention is centred, not on Sir Aylmer and his wife but upon their daughter Edith and her young lover Leolin Averill, the story is a tragedy of a different sort, a romantic tragedy of young love destroyed in its innocence. A third minor tragedy, again of a different sort, is embodied in the story of the older Averill, his hopes for his younger brother, and his sermon at the funeral. This is in part a tragedy of revenge, but not simply so; the character of Averill as developed by Tennyson is made more complex than any other in the story.

The problem presented by the facts, then, is that they are

capable of too many sorts of development. A unified treatment would be possible. It is obvious that Tennyson could have told the story of Sir Aylmer Aylmer, concentrating solely on his intentions and actions, presenting the wayward behaviour of his daughter and Leolin as it appears to him, showing in detail what thoughts passed through his mind during the sermon, keeping always the stories of the young lovers and of the Averills carefully subordinate and ancillary. Even in doing this he would have had a choice of tones. He could have used throughout a plain and detached style, seeming to let the facts speak for themselves, or he could have used a dry ironic style, presenting the tragedy with a note of savage implied comment. Or again, he could have told the story of the young lovers in the high style of romantic tragedy, keeping Sir Aylmer lightly sketched in but never central, just as in *Romeo and Juliet* the antagonism of the Capulets and Montagues is present as a cause of the tragedy but not itself developed as a theme. Any one of these treatments, handled in a uniform style suitable to its genre, would have resulted in a tightly organized poem creating a powerful single effect.

What Tennyson chose to do, however, was to include in one poem all these disparate types of development. It is small wonder that he found such difficulty in writing it, as he is constantly faced with fresh decisions as to the most suitable style and tone of particular passages. He uses a great variety of styles. The poem opens with a solemn moral, couched in a dignified high style:

> Dust are our frames; and, gilded dust, our pride
> Looks only for a moment whole and sound;
> Like that long-buried body of the king,
> Found lying with his urns and ornaments,
> Which at a touch of light, an air of heaven,
> Slipt into ashes, and was found no more.

The description of Sir Aylmer and his wife a few lines later moves towards the scornful irony which is to be attached to them through the main part of the poem:

> Sir Aylmer Aylmer, that almighty man,
> The county God . . .
> His wife a faded beauty of the Baths,
> Insipid as the Queen upon a card;
> Her all of thought and bearing hardly more
> Than his own shadow in a sickly sun.

The Averills, and Leolin in particular, are described, as is Edith, in romantic style, filled with allusions to the beauties of the natural world. Leolin is described:

> Sanguine he was: a but less vivid hue
> Than of that islet in the chestnut-bloom
> Flamed in his cheek; and eager eyes, that still
> Took joyful note of all things joyful, beamed,
> Beneath a manelike mass of rolling gold . . . .

The two styles, one for Sir Aylmer, one for the young lovers, create a sense of two opposed worlds, two kinds of life, two sets of values, two kinds of persons. The one is the world of Mammon, seeking wealth and power, insensitive to beauty, guarded and circumspect; the other the world of Love, spontaneous, eager, full of beauty, taking 'joyful note of all things joyful', child-like in its charming openness and warmth. The one world is the world of the county, of the Baths, of Court; the other the world of the fresh countryside.

The depiction of the world of young love is always in the high romantic style, with elaborations and enrichments quite in Tennyson's early manner. Leolin, as a ten-year-old orphan, 'for want of playmates' plays with the little five-year-old Edith, he

> Had tost his ball and flown his kite, and rolled
> His hoop to pleasure Edith, with her dipt
> Against the rush of air in the prone swing . . .
> Showed her the fairy footings on the grass,
> The little dells of cowslips, fairy palms,
> The pretty marestail forest, fairy pines,
> Or from the tiny pitted target blew
> What looked a flight of fairy arrows aimed
> All at one mark, all hitting . . .

The repetitions of 'fairy', the close child's view of minute nature, suggest steadily the eye of the child, the poet, the lover, seeing magic and mystery in beauty. The children, and later the lovers, are 'a couple, fair As ever painter painted, poet sang, Or Heaven in lavish bounty moulded. . . .' The world of Sir Aylmer at the Hall is a world of 'dull sameness', the Baronet himself,

> dull and self-involved,
> Tall and erect, but bending from his height
> With half-allowing smiles for all the world,

And mighty courteous in the main – his pride
Lay deeper than to wear it as his ring –
He, like an Aylmer in his Aylmerism . . .

The style here, unlike that applied to the children and lovers, is
not exuberant, flowing, crowded with rich details, vivid touches
of description, and as it were quivering with spontaneous delight
and excitement; it is tight in structure, abstract, and conveying
more by implication than by elaboration. Sir Aylmer's smiles are
'for all the world': They convey, and are meant to convey, no
personal warmth, no sense of his amusement or joy, they are
simply an external mark of polite condescension, available to all.
They are 'half-allowing' smiles: they invite no liberties of friendship or companionship; they preserve the other half ('forbidding').
The Baronet's height, from which he bends when he sees fit, is
strongly contrasted with the close-to-earth point of view of the
young lovers, their eager eyes ranging over the world's beauty,
their smiles expressing their unselfconscious joy and love.

Tennyson uses his immense stylistic resources to set these two
worlds against each other; often, as here, in a quickly alternating
pattern, in much the same way as a composer will set up and
develop two contrasting themes, each with its instrumental
tonality and texture, each carrying its own associations of mood
and implications. The technique is also like the dramatic use of
contrasting scenes, such as Shakespeare's alternation in *Henry V*
of views of the French and English camps before Agincourt, or
his contrasts of Egypt and Rome in *Antony and Cleopatra*. Tennyson's structure is perhaps closer to the musical analogy than to the
dramatic, being more fluid and not tied specifically to action.
Much of the writing, in fact, suggests a musical composition,
creating its effect at least as much by tonality and by suggestion
as by the explicit and literal meaning. Such passages are often
extended far beyond the demands of narration or exposition,
detail after detail contributing, not to our understanding of events,
or characters, or even of necessary setting, but building up a kind
of tone-poem with accompanying symbolic suggestions.

The method can only be seen fully in one of the long and
elaborate passages, but some illustration can be given in a
short extract from one of them. The complete passage, lines 144
to 188 in the poem, relates Edith's first becoming half aware of
her love for Leolin when, on one of her charitable visits to the

labourers' cottages, accompanied this time by Leolin, she hears one
of the labourers' wives whisper, 'God bless 'em: marriages are
made in Heaven'. This narrative content, as a contribution to the
action of the story, takes up not much more than half a dozen of
the forty-four lines. The rest is essentially the sort of musical
elaboration defined above. The passage follows a shorter one on
the young lovers, describing their 'young hearts' as they 'wandered
at will', bound 'by an immemorial intimacy', 'wandered, hour by
hour Gathered the blossoms that rebloomed, and drank The
magic cup that filled itself anew'.

> A whisper half revealed her to herself.
> For out beyond her lodges, where the brook
> Vocal, with here and there a silence, ran
> By sallowy rims, arose the labourers' homes,
> A frequent haunt of Edith, on low knolls
> That dimpling died into each other, huts
> At random scattered, each a nest in bloom.
> . . . Here was one that, summer-blanched,
> Was parcel-bearded with the traveller's joy
> In Autumn, parcel ivy-clad; and here
> The warm-blue breathings of a hidden hearth
> Broke from a bower of vine and honeysuckle:
> One looked all rosetree, and another wore
> A close-set robe of jasmine sown with stars:
> This had a rosy sea of gillyflowers
> About it; this, a milky-way on earth,
> Like visions in the Northern dreamer's heavens,
> A lily-avenue climbing to the doors;
> One, almost to the martin-haunted eaves
> A summer burial deep in hollyhocks;
> Each, its own charm; and Edith's everywhere . . .

A melodious passage, and how thickly set with suggestive images!
The effect is that of Pope and Handel's 'Where'er you walk' – the
strong sense of beauty and goodness almost divine at whose
presence flowers spring up and all life bursts into bloom, and all is
secure. Together the cottages form a 'bower', the 'frequent
haunt' of Edith, whose 'charm is everywhere'. The brook, the
'dimpling' knolls, the 'nest in bloom', 'traveller's joy', 'warm-
blue breathings', 'hidden hearth', 'broke from a bower', 'close-
set robe', 'summer burial', 'sown with stars', 'rosy sea' (with its

vision of Venus), 'milky-way on earth', 'Northern dreamer's heavens' – how the suggestions and associations by their cumulative power create the evocative quality of the lines! All is insinuated by sound and suggestion and symbol; this is not a set, visualized landscape with each cottage in its place – the images succeed each other so rapidly that each flashes on the mind only long enough to make an instant's vision. The pace is not that of Edith, walking from cottage to cottage; it is like that of a fast train giving sudden glimpses of idyllic tiny landscapes.

The dramatic action develops swiftly after this passage; one verse paragraph describes the arrival of 'My lady's Indian kinsman', Leolin's 'semi-jealousy' which makes Edith fully recognize her love for him; another two paragraphs the jewelled dagger the kinsman presents to Edith and her giving it to Leolin, which Sir Aylmer notes and 'neither loved nor liked the thing he heard'. The next paragraph brings a gossipy neighbour to drop Sir Aylmer a hint that he should watch Edith and Leolin, and Sir Aylmer's storm of fury follows at once. For these rapid developments, the style is again modified to a swift dramatic narrative, with quick snatches of conversation, direct or reported. After the deliberately slow tempo of the opening, the sense of the static and timeless in the formalized world of Sir Aylmer and in the idyllic natural world of Edith and Leolin, the quick movement towards tragedy suggests the ruin of both worlds. First to be destroyed is the cold, urbane, and polished world of formal civility Sir Aylmer has constructed. We see him changed instantly, his façade broken through. And with the change, Tennyson drops the cool, ironic style appropriate to the façade. Now Sir Aylmer is described as 'glaring, by his own stale devil spurred, And, like a beast hard-ridden, breathing hard'. 'Reddening from the storm within', he 'broke all bonds of courtesy', stammering 'out of teeth that ground As in a dreadful dream', and finally 'under his own lintel stood Storming with lifted hands', his face 'Vext with unworthy madness, and deformed'. The style now applied to Sir Aylmer, with its emphasis on demonic possession and madness, not only emphasizes the destruction of his formal *persona*, but also in its change of tone marks a change in our point of view. The cool ironic style at first used for Sir Aylmer focussed our attention on the first theme, of the man of high place and power ironically destroying himself through *hubris*. Now we see Sir Aylmer as the demonic force of evil destroying the idyllic and innocent world of the young lovers. The move to this second theme of the story, with its accompanying strong emotional involvement, is managed mainly through selection of style. Continuance of the earlier ironic style would have put emphasis on Sir Aylmer's folly, on the irony of the poised and cool aristocrat losing his poise and falling into 'outrageous epithets' like a Billingsgate porter, but not on the satanic, the brutal, the savage.

The tone and style applied to the lovers now also changes, since their world is also shattered. They are presented now in terms of the pathetic, and this is conveyed, not through the ornate style, but through the simple:

> Yet once by night again the lovers met,
> A perilous meeting under the tall pines
> That darkened all the northward of her Hall . . .
>   So they talked,
> Poor children, for their comfort: the wind blew;
> The rain of heaven, and their own bitter tears,
> Tears, and the careless rain of heaven, mixt
> Upon their faces, as they kissed each other
> In darkness, and above them roared the pine.

The symbolism is still present, the dark, the northward, the rain, the 'careless rain', and the roaring cold wind – the landscape and weather form a contrast with the paradisal scenes of their early meetings – but diction and style are simple, imagery restrained, for an effect of pathetic, dignified suffering.

At this meeting, Leolin resolved to return to London to continue his studies of the law, in the hope of succeeding so well that he might appear to Sir Aylmer a suitable match for Edith. The passage describing his studies is one of those which, Tennyson says, gave him most trouble to write. The problem was no doubt structural and stylistic, since the one involves the other. A description of Leolin's studies is hardly necessary to the telling of the dramatic story, but if it is included, how is it to be used? The state of Leolin's mind, trying to master the remote intricacies of ancient cases with the immediate urgency of his and Edith's present situation pressing on him, is an obvious concern, but what state should his mind be in? And what style suits? His mood could be seen as pathetic, or as one of savage frustration, as one of despair at ever mastering a subject so aridly academic while his real interest and anxieties lay elsewhere. Tennyson finally made a brilliant choice by deciding to balance this paragraph with the following one describing events at the Hall. And the theme of each paragraph is hope: Leolin's hope of restoring the lost world of love, and the Aylmers' hope of restoring their artificial world. The earlier tones and styles are consequently partly reintroduced into the paragraphs, but only momentarily: Leolin runs beside the river-bank during a brief respite from his studies, and

> the soft river-breeze,
> Which fanned the gardens of that rival rose
> Yet fragrant in a heart remembering
> His former talks with Edith, on him breathed
> Far purelier in his rushing to and fro . . .

While at the Hall,

> They that cast her spirit into flesh,
> Her worldly-wise begetters, plagued themselves
> To sell her, those good parents, for her good.
> Whatever eldest-born of rank or wealth
> Might lie within their compass, him they lured
> Into their net made pleasant by the baits
> Of gold and beauty, wooing him to woo.

These reminiscences of the earlier tones, the idyllic and the ironic, sustain briefly the pattern of the opening sections of the poem, but the later tone of tragedy rapidly returns: as Edith ruins the Aylmers' plans by rejecting suitor after suitor,

> Those at home,
> As hunters round a hunted creature draw
> The cordon close and closer toward the death,
> Narrowed her goings out and comings in . . .

The death of the hunted Edith follows soon after. But just before the lines recording her death, and set between descriptions of the Aylmers' cruelty, is the brief but significant account of Sir Aylmer's display of his real but unconscious affection for Edith:

> once indeed
> Warmed with his wines, or taking pride in her,
> She looked so sweet, he kissed her tenderly
> Not knowing what possessed him . . .
> and then ensued
> A Martin's summer of his faded love,
> Or ordeal by kindness . . .

Until the last phrase, these lines recall neither the ironic nor the
demonic; they suggest a literal, rather than ironic interpretation
of 'those good parents, for her good', or at least an interpretation
in which the irony is that of misjudgement rather than of hypo-
crisy. And the word 'pride', in 'taking pride in her', implies a
different sort of pride from that so far linked with the Aylmers.
Again, the direct simplicity of the style at this point, with its
implication of an unrealized and unconscious sincerity in Sir
Aylmer, prepares for a readjustment of our view of him.

The suicide of Leolin is told very rapidly after Edith's death –
in a mere twenty-one lines. It is narrated in a curiously oblique
way, possibly to avoid too much emphasis on the fact that it *is*
suicide, and also to leave Leolin's state of mind, sound or un-
sound, in doubt. Most of the short passage is used to suggest
that he has joined his dead love: at the moment of her death, as
she cried out his name, 'the keen shriek "Yes love, yes, Edith,
yes"', shrilled, and Leolin rose,

> His body half flung forward in pursuit,
> And his long arms stretched as to grasp a flyer:
> Nor knew he wherefore he had made the cry . . .

The second day after, he is found with the letter informing him of
Edith's death, and the implication is that he has understood his
dream and answered the call.

Thus ends the tragedy of the young lovers, and Tennyson
returns to the Aylmer parents. Roughly a third of the poem takes
us to the beginning of Sir Aylmer's first outburst of fury, the next
third to the death of the lovers. The last third describes the funeral
sermon, the deaths of the parents, and the fates of the Aylmers and
their Hall. And once more Tennyson modifies the style and tone.
The setting itself, the village, is no longer filled with life and
colour:

> Darkly that day rose:
> Autumn's mock sunshine of the faded woods
> Was all the life of it; for hard on these,
> A breathless burthen of low-folded heavens
> Stifled and chilled at once . . .

How superbly apt is the image of Autumn's 'mock sunshine' – the warm yellows, bronzes and browns of the fallen leaves beneath the bare trees create an illusion of golden sunlight in the rain-soaked woods, mockingly suggesting life where there is no life. In this symbolic setting, and in a church 'one night, except for greenish glimmerings through the lancets', Averill delivers his funeral sermon.

The sermon dominates this last part of the poem, taking up two-thirds of its lines, continuing with what seems remorseless persistence. At a superficial level, and contemplated simply within the context of the dramatic action of the story as a story, the sermon must seem an understandable but nonetheless dreadful act of cruelty. The Aylmers, in strict justice, deserve every word of condemnation in it, and Averill's own life, shattered with his brother's, has had little enough of love in it to help him now be largely charitable. But for a clergyman to exploit the text suggested by the mother of the dead girl by giving it a tone and meaning she had not anticipated, for him to turn the funeral of a dead daughter into a savage attack on her parents, seems essentially shocking. A closer examination of the sermon, however, dispels simple judgements. The sermon opens indeed with a dreadful denunciation, as Averill 'dashed his angry heart Against the desolations of the world'. For twenty lines he attacks the worship of Baäl, of the god 'diffused in noble groves And princely halls, and farms, and flowing lawns, And heaps of living gold that daily grow, And title-scrolls and gorgeous heraldries'. Then he sets against this worship that of Christ, the 'One who cried, "Leave all and follow me"'. From this he turns to a depiction of Edith as exemplar of the Christian life, 'for she walked Wearing the light yoke of that Lord of love, Who stilled the rolling wave of Galilee'. These passages, of some sixty-five lines, three times as long as the opening denunciation, are filled, not with anger, but with love and pity. The style of them is noble, touched with the lyrical. From Edith he turns for a moment to Leolin, – 'of him I was not bid to speak' – a touch of bitterness here, but still the dominant tone is one of deep sorrow, not of indignation. At this point Tennyson interrupts the sermon for a brief glance, twelve lines long, at the Aylmers, noting the effect on them of Averill's words. His opening attack has merely roused Sir Aylmer's anger, so that he sat, 'anger-charmed from sorrow, Soldierlike, erect', but when the preacher's 'cadence flowed'

> Softening through all the gentle attributes
> Of his lost child, the wife, who watched his face,
> Paled at a sudden twitch of his iron mouth;
> And 'O pray God that he hold up' she thought
> 'Or surely I shall shame myself and him.'

This passage, short as it is, is of great importance in the structure at this point. For the first time in the poem, it describes the Aylmers in direct, simple style, with no ironic tone, and with no suggestion of their monstrosity. It emphasizes ordinary human feelings in them: the twitch of Sir Aylmer's iron mouth, the threat to the iron composure which is part of his pride, comes this time not from fury, but from pity and sorrow. And the sudden glimpse of the wife's feelings, most brilliantly suggested by the one sentence, complex in its implications, of her thoughts, suddenly makes her something other than a vacant 'Queen upon a card'. At this moment, then, Tennyson turns our attention from Averill to the Aylmers, making us at the same time aware of them in a new way, as parents at their only daughter's funeral, struggling to preserve a stoical dignity threatened by their real sorrow.

As the sermon continues, it resumes the mode of the prophets, but the tone of anger, of the prophet calling down the wrath of God, surges up only briefly. The dominant tone is set in most powerful terms of prayer and pity: Averill asks for the prayers of his congregation, for he himself is 'lonelier, darker, earthlier', for his loss, and he feels now that his anger itself is vileness and pride. And the sermon ends with a most moving prayer:

> O rather pray for those and pity them,
> Who, through their own desire accomplished, bring
> Their own gray hairs with sorrow to the grave . . .
> Who wove coarse webs to snare her purity,
> Grossly contriving their dear daughter's good –
> Poor souls, and knew not what they did, but sat
> Ignorant, devising their own daughter's death!

The prayer of Christ, 'Father, forgive them, for they know not what they do', the repentance for his own anger, the tremendous sense of pity for the Aylmers reflected especially in Averill's reference to himself as 'their guest, their host, their ancient friend', forced by his very love for them to speak out to save them, to save all those who swear 'not by the temple but the

gold' – these characterize the ending of the sermon, the ending
towards which it is dramatically directed. The sermon is an act of
purgation for Averill: it begins in anger and hate and ends in
pity and love. In thus purging his own spirit of those qualities
which he has come to recognize as themselves part of an earthly
pride, Averill has brought himself to the path of Christian love, or
charity, the path Edith (and perhaps also Leolin) had always
walked.

By implication, Tennyson, too, is rejecting anger and hate, and
with it the bitter tone applied earlier to the Aylmers. The poem
itself, like the sermon, is a progression, an illustration of the
Christian way towards love. It is no accident that the divine
associations attached to Edith in the early part of the poem, some
of which we noted, are all pagan, of Diana of the grove, of Venus
rising from the sea, and her love and Leolin's is described in
terms of earthly love, of romance. Now at the end there are divine
associations, but all Christian and angelic: Edith is 'Fair as the
Angel that said "Hail!"' at the Annunciation, 'who entering
filled the house with sudden light.' Her

> fresh and innocent eyes
> Had such a star of morning in their blue,
> That all neglected places of the field
> Broke into nature's music when they saw her....
> 'Had you ... One burthen and she would not lighten it?
> One spiritual doubt she did not soothe?'

There has been through the poem a movement from physical to
spiritual, from earthly to heavenly, from secular love to spiritual
love, from a story of the tragedy of the frustration of secular love to
that of the deeper tragedy for Tennyson of the denial of divine love.

The style with which Tennyson consequently describes our last
sight of the Aylmers, as they leave the church, the wife unconscious, carried along the nave by her servants, and Sir Aylmer,

> Tall and erect, but in the middle aisle
> Reeled, as a footsore ox in crowded ways
> Stumbling across the market to his death,
> Unpitied; for he groped as blind, and seemed
> Always about to fall, grasping the pews
> And oaken finials till he touched the door;
> Yet to the lychgate where his chariot stood,
> Strode from the porch, tall and erect again.

is a style filled with pity, and also with a sense of the dignity of suffering endured. The pride that keeps Sir Aylmer 'tall and erect' is a different thing from his pride in possession, power, and high lineage, – it is like Lear's 'Nay, I'll not weep'.

The coda is short, and ends with powerful simplicity:

> Then the great Hall was wholly broken down,
> And the broad woodland parcelled into farms;
> And where the two contrived their daughter's good,
> Lies the hawk's cast, the mole has made his run,
> The hedgehog underneath the plantain bores,
> The rabbit fondles his own harmless face,
> The slow-worm creeps, and the thin weasel there
> Follows the mouse, and all is open field.

There is of course here the theme of the fallen mighty, of Shelley's *Ozymandias*, but the details of the life of nature carry further suggestions, particularly the emphatic place given the predatory weasel and his prey, the mouse. The predatory is part of Nature. But the predatory in man is a denial of his highest nature, a denial of love. The Hall fell through the Aylmer's dedication to the code of the predator; it has properly returned to the sphere of the predatory.

From the 'dry facts' given him by Woolner, Tennyson has created an extremely complex poem. It fuses at least three traditional genres, or rather moves from one to the other, changing styles accordingly, conveying much of its meaning through the changes. The technique is an interesting, original and demanding one; what it demands above all is a sense of how in various genres diction, syntax, imagery, and in fact all the elements of the style create associations and emotional attitudes in the reader. No poet has a better ear for the nuances and suggestions of style than Tennyson, and no other poet has put his skill to work in quite this manner, where the mixture of styles becomes itself a major element in poetic structure.

CHAPTER 4

The Creation of new Genres:
Maud, In Memoriam, Idylls of the King

𝕊𝕊𝕊𝕊𝕊𝕊

As we have seen, the Classical and Romantic conceptions of genre differ – for the Classical or neo-Classical poet, genre is something to be defined and created in pure form, using its appropriate kind of language as medium, with decorum, or a sense of fitness, as guide; while for the Romantic poet genre is more like a set of effects, a texture, a restricted palette, a pattern of tonalities, to use at the poet's discretion in new combinations. The shift of critical attention from the work of art as a formal structure, from which rules of structure might be discovered, to the psychological and aesthetic effect of the work on its audience, from the art object to its viewing subject, no doubt accounts in part for the change in attitude towards genre. We have traced some of Tennyson's experiments in genre in the preceding chapter, from relatively minor innovations to highly unorthodox blends and fusions. We must now consider, necessarily briefly, three major works whose structure is so radically different from anything written before that each virtually creates its own new genre. Needless to say, the introduction of a new genre is a hazardous undertaking for the poet, since the critic is likely to attempt to judge it in terms of the old familiar genres. He asks at the outset, 'What sort of poem is this?', reviewing his known categories; and when it fails to fit any of them, or the one he has decided it ought to fit, is prone to condemn it as a failure. The three works to be discussed here have all suffered at some time or another, and to varying extents, from this sort of misjudgement. One cannot entirely blame the critics, since the use of any aspect of a traditional genre, of its structure, its tonalities, its level of diction, its kind of syntax, at once calls up the whole defined nature of that genre, and it is indeed this pattern of defined associations that the poet is exploiting. His fundamental problem is to make the associations selective, but not complete.

Maud is perhaps the most obviously revolutionary in technique and conception of Tennyson's poems. He calls it a 'monodrama' – which tells us only what we can readily perceive: That the theme is a dramatic one, and there is only one speaker. The implications are however very important, and not always fully realized. They can best be brought out by a comparison of *Maud* with ordinary drama as presented on a stage, and since Tennyson himself suggested some similarity to *Hamlet* in the poem, *Hamlet* will serve for comparison. What ought to strike us at once, if we read *Maud* without preconceptions carried over from our familiarity with ordinary drama, is that the question raised by Dover Wilson, of '*what happens in Hamlet?*' is a very different one from 'what happens in *Maud?*' Wilson is not asking questions about the physical action, about whether Hamlet did indeed thrust his sword through the arras and kill Polonius, whether Ophelia drowned herself, or whether Hamlet wrestled in the grave of Ophelia with Laertes. We are certain of the whole pattern of physical, external events; what we question is the area we cannot fully penetrate, the area of psychological event. We do not know precisely what is happening in Hamlet's mind. We know what he says and what he does in, say, the cellarage scene, but how to read his state of mind? And the dramatic effect is obviously not dependent upon any certainty about the inner psychological event; as long as our speculations about their nature can be made to cohere with the fixed pattern of external event and spoken utterance, a dramatic pattern is preserved, so that we can have a number of *Hamlets*, identical in text and physical action, but varying from an 'active' *Hamlet* in which the psychological is subordinated to the physical action, to the 'introspective' *Hamlet* in which the action is subordinated to the psychological.

In *Maud*, we have something like a complete reversal of this situation. What we are certain of is the inner action, what the hero thinks – and the drama is created in the inner psychological action. This is what Tennyson suggested when he said 'The peculiarity of this poem is that different phases of passion in one person take the place of different characters'. We have in fact no way of establishing the physical events, of knowing 'what happened' in physical fact. We have no way of knowing that the hero did actually fight a duel, and kill Maud's brother; we know his mind is unsettled and full of fantasies: his disordered imagination and his fears could have produced a nightmare delusion which is, of course, as real to him as reality. There is no objective link to an outside world; we are confined throughout to the recesses of one strange mind. The reader is so habituated to ordinary drama that he tends to keep asking 'what really happened?' and to seek an objective reality to cling to; it takes a conscious effort to break the habit. The conscious effort is worth making in the case of *Maud*, to allow the reader to grasp its essential nature, which is that of a self-contained psychological drama. Once this is grasped, the reader can, if he wishes, admit the objective reality of external events in the action if they seem necessary; but it is important to start by understanding that it does not matter whether Maud's father had anything to do with the death of the hero's father; it does not matter whether there are rival suitors for Maud's hand; or whether the hero and Maud's brother actually had a quarrel. These things may be actualities, but we have no way of knowing that they are; what we *do* know is that they are actualities in the hero's mind: he *thought* all these things, and his thoughts are the only certain reality in the drama. The dramatic pattern and the powerful dramatic effect of the poem do not depend on any external reality; it scarcely makes any difference to the drama *as drama* whether the hero actually killed Maud's brother or only thought he did.

Where it will make a difference will be in our view or interpretation of the relation of the hero's thought to what we suppose to be objective reality of action; a kind of opposite process to that by which we try to relate the physical action of *Hamlet* to what we suppose to be its hero's states of mind. In the latter case we start with known objective action and move from it to psychology; in the former we start with known states of mind and move from them to action, for the action in *Maud* proceeds from the state of mind of the hero, insofar as we are sure there *is* action. The ending, for example, since it convinces us that the hero has recovered his sanity, convinces us that the action he describes, going to war, is real. But this action does not result from the previous pattern of physical action, but from the pattern of his psychological movement, and it is totally wrong to look at going to war as a physical action in the usual way, bringing in thoughts of one's own about war, and judging the meaning of it in *Maud* from these thoughts; the meaning of this and all the other actions here is dependent, not on what the reader thinks of them as actions, but on what the hero thinks. The whole fundamental dramatic action is contained in the hero's mind. The conflict and irony which form the basis of dramatic action, and which in ordinary drama are created by external action, by external situations, by the clash of external characters or forces, are here created internally, as Tennyson indicates.

It is not surprising that the structure of *Maud* bears little superficial resemblance to that of conventional drama. The skeletal structure, or gross anatomy, of stage drama is nearly always an arrangement of physical actions, as the term 'acts' implies. It is also presented through dialogue, spoken by the characters engaged in the action, usually in defined settings of place and time. The very substance of this kind of drama, the usual kind, is a strong sense of objective reality and of immediacy. The audience is looking directly at characters acting and speaking. What is most interesting about the technique of *Maud* is the deliberate exclusion of this sort of objective immediacy. Tennyson was certainly not incapable of it; his conventional plays, particularly *Queen Mary* and *Becket*, are extremely successful, and he preceded Browning as a master of the dramatic monologue. He could obviously have composed *Maud* as a conventional drama, or as a series of dramatic monologues in which other characters appear as *mutae personae* whose dialogue has been temporarily suspended. This latter is the technique Browning so often uses, and by which he makes us as immediately and physically aware of Lucrezia as of Andrea del Sarto, of Gigadibs as of Bishop Blougram, of the Duchess as of the Duke. It is a technique that fully preserves the sense, as in stage drama, of the spectator's presence at the very moment of conflict, and preserves also the sense of the physical reality of the setting, of an external objective world of objects and of other persons. To recall this technique is useful; it illuminates what *Maud* is by reminding us of what it is not.

For Tennyson keeps the sense of location in space and time generally vague or unspecified; we seldom know with any degree of exactness where the hero is or how much time has elapsed from section to section. The most important settings, the little wood and Maud's garden, are not given the sharply-focused physical reality we find in Browning's settings, or in most of Tennyson's. They exist as symbols, and in association with sets of ideas and emotions in the hero's mind, rather than as physical places for physical action. We cannot be sure that the hero is, in the second part, actually immured; if he is, we have certainly no physical conception of the institution or place of confinement. The events which we may assume to have taken place in the world of external reality are all given to us as the hero's reminiscences; we are always at a remove from them in time and place. What we have instead is an immediacy of another order: what is always immediately present to us is a mind, a reality indeed, but a psychological reality not simply located in space and time. The action which is immediately present to us is the movement of this mind, and this it is which constitutes the 'dramatic action'.

It is of course true that internal conflict and psychological movement are often of great – often, some would say, of primary – importance in conventional drama. But there the inner action takes place in a total pattern of external action, and much of the conflict is expressed in external action. In *Hamlet* and *Othello*, for example, the King and Iago initiate much of the action, and the internal movement follows the external as much as it leads it. In *Maud*, on the contrary, the primary movement is all internal, the conflicts are internal. In place of opposed characters, we start with opposed mental forces within the same mind, and the drama is created by the struggle of these forces. The patterned structure of the poem is not a patterned structure of complex physical action, but of these forces: on the one side, hate, fear, distrust, despair, selfishness, death; on the other, love, courage, trust, faith, deliverance from self, and life. Everything in the hero's mind is associated with these elements of the conflict; everything becomes a symbol. The dramatic movement is made up of shifts and modulations in the grouping of these elements in the hero's mind, and, as in conventional drama, many of the modulations are ironic. The fundamental movement, as is usual, is from an initial situation full of unresolved conflict towards a resolution – both here internal and psychological – but the movement is not simply linear, nor unambiguous: the reader comes to know the hero's mind better than the hero knows it himself, just as in stage drama the audience sees more of the significance of actions than the characters do, and can sense the irony of their actions. Here we can sense, for example, just before the catastrophe, the note of instability in the hero's frame of mind that warns us that the total triumphant resolution that he thinks is achieved is infinitely fragile: he is not, as he thinks, firmly planted on secure ground, but precariously poised on a knife-edge. It is this balance of his mind that we watch with anxiety, with hopes and fears and ironic forebodings, not his actions or deeds.

Structurally, the two most basic symbols are the little wood and Maud's garden. The poem opens: 'I hate the dreadful hollow behind the little wood': it is associated with hate, dread, bloodshed, and death. It is linked, as the place where the hero's father died, with memories of his corpse, 'mangled, and flattened, and crush'd, and dinted into the ground', with the shock and fear of his death, with thoughts of his wife's terrible grief, and with all the implications concerning a cut-throat competitive society raised by the failure in business which, the hero thinks, caused his father's death. The little wood thus expands into a symbol of a whole world of moral disorder, of an anarchic predatory Nature:

For Nature is one with rapine, a harm no preacher can heal;
The Mayfly is torn by the swallow, the sparrow speared by the shrike,
And the whole little wood where I sit is a world of plunder and prey.

The hero sees human society in terms of this Nature, where each man preys on his fellows, dominated by the 'lust of gain, in the spirit of Cain'. He sees himself at first as belonging in the little wood, accepting cynically and savagely the gladiatorial law of 'kill or be killed'. He promises himself that he will acquire a hard indifference, to 'bury himself in himself'. But he cannot forget the reality of his mother's love for his father, nor the beauty and charm of Maud as a child, and these memories stir in him the emotions he would deny.

These emotions come to centre in Maud, and become grouped around the symbol of the garden, which becomes Maud's world as the little wood is the hero's. Maud's is the world of moral order, of beauty, of life, of courage, love, and purity:

> Maud has a garden of roses
> And lilies fair on a lawn;
> There she walks in her state
> And tends upon bed and bower,
> And thither I climb'd at dawn
> And stood by her garden-gate;
> A lion ramps at the top,
> He is claspt by a passion-flower.

Roses and lilies, symbols of love and purity, of the Virgin; the enclosed garden with its suggestions of an Eden and of man's pre-fallen state; the lion, symbol of nobility and courage, 'claspt by a passion-flower', symbol of Christ's suffering and sacrifice – all gather into a rich and complex pattern of significance.

Underlying the contrasted symbols of the wood and the garden is the theme T. H. Huxley was to recognize and use in his *Evolution and Ethics*, the theme presented by Tennyson in *In Memoriam* in the question, 'Are God and Nature then at strife?' Since Huxley believes in neither God nor Nature he has to put his question in terms of what he calls the Ethical Process and the Cosmic Process, using the garden to symbolize the first, and the wild heath for the second. Huxley finds that they are and must be at strife, accepting a dichotomized world, as does Thomas Hardy in his more tragic moods, seeing the Ethical Process as a futile man-made struggle against the dominant amoral and mindless Cosmic Process. Through the two main symbols, then, *Maud* raises the cosmic question of all great tragedy.

The main movement of the poem is conveyed through the interplay of these central symbols, the symbols of the two worlds, as the hero's mind is torn between them. He yearns towards the world of the garden, wishing that he could believe in its reality and often willing to believe; his fears and doubts pull him back towards the world of the wood. As he comes to admit to himself his love for Maud, and to put trust in her love for him, he moves more completely into the world of order, until at moments he sees only one world; his own world of the wood becomes part of the garden, and is no longer 'my own dark wood', but 'our wood'. And at the full avowal of love (in section XVIII of part one) the wood becomes an Eden like the garden:

> O, art thou sighing for Lebanon
> In the long breeze that streams to thy delicious East,
> Sighing for Lebanon,
> Dark cedar, though thy limbs have here increased,
> Upon a pastoral slope as fair,
> And looking to the South, and fed
> With honey'd rain and delicate air,
> And haunted by the starry head
> Of her whose gentle will has changed my fate,
> And made my life a perfumed altar-flame;

> And over whom thy darkness must have spread
> With such delight as theirs of old, thy great
> Forefathers, of the thornless garden, there
> Shadowing the snow-limb'd Eve from whom she came.

The rivulet that runs from the Hall to the wood becomes a symbolic link; it carries down from Maud's garden one of the roses, bringing into the wood part of the world of the garden.

The catastrophe is brought about by a true *peripeteia*, a reverse movement. The hero's effort to bury hate, to suppress the world of the wood or transform it, fails in a sudden uprush of anger and pride. This is represented by action in the garden, which itself is now invaded by the world of the wood, the world of hate and death:

> O dawn of Eden bright over earth and sky,
> The fires of Hell broke out of thy rising sun,
> The fires of Hell and of Hate . . .

Death itself follows in 'the red-ribbed hollow behind the wood', and the world of the garden is destroyed:

> But I know where a garden grows,
> Fairer than aught in the world beside,
> All made up of the lily and rose
> That blow by night, when the season is good,
> To the sound of dancing music and flutes:
> It is only flowers, they had no fruits,
> And I almost fear they are not roses, but blood;
> For the keeper was one, so full of pride,
> He linkt a dead man there to a spectral bride.

This broad movement, from the opening in which hate and death are dominant, to the apparent triumph of life and love, followed by the reversal of the catastrophe, then through the hero's madness to the final resolution, is not of course simple. As in all true drama, the tension between the two forces is always there, and the usual devices of irony and of preshadowing or foreboding keep us constantly aware of the delicate balance upon which the outcome depends. In conventional drama, incidents or situations can be ambiguous; here ambiguity is found not only in states of mind but in some of the symbols.

The most important ambiguity attaches to Peace and War: this is an ambiguity essential to the pattern of the conclusion. From the beginning of the poem to the end, the hero constantly thinks of peace in terms of the world of the wood, a world of ruthlessness, a society in which every hand is turned against every other, and in which the lives of others are readily sacrificed for selfish gain. A society at peace he sees only as one in a state of undeclared civil war, and stained with dishonour and cowardice. War he associates with Maud, with courage, and with abnegation of self in sacrifice. He first hears Maud singing

> A passionate ballad gallant and gay,
> A martial song like a trumpet's call! . . .
> Maud in the light of her youth and her grace,
> Singing of Death, and of Honour that cannot die . . .

Her song is 'the chivalrous battle-song That she warbled alone in her joy'. Henceforth his thoughts of War are linked tightly with thoughts of Maud and her song, with 'the happy morning of life and of May', with gay and noble resolve, with Honour in death in an unselfish cause. He distinguishes between 'lawful and lawless war', the first being in a public cause for unselfish ends, the second being 'the red life spilt for a private blow'. It is consequently entirely in character, and consonant with the whole dramatic pattern, that he should turn from the ignoble private war exemplified in his father's death and his own duel with Maud's brother to the public war in which he can offer himself in sacrifice. This is his return from the wood to the garden, as his final image indicates – he seeks 'the blood-red blossom of war with a heart of fire'. He breaks out from the prison of self, frees his 'heart of stone', climbs 'nearer out of lonely Hell' to be 'one with his kind'. It is a vision of Maud that assists him to his decision; the ending of the drama is implicit in its beginning. Related ambiguities are found in his thoughts on death. He finds himself ready to die for Maud: he 'would die to save from some slight shame one simple girl':

> Would die; for sullen-seeming Death may give
> More life to Love than is or ever was
> In our low world, where yet 'tis sweet to live.
> . . . 'The dusky strand of Death inwoven here
> With dear Love's tie, makes Love himself more dear.'

His great song of triumph, 'Come into the garden, Maud', reaches its climactic finale in a vision of such a Life-in-Death of love:

> She is coming, my own, my sweet;
>   Were it ever so airy a tread,
> My heart would hear her and beat,
>   Were it earth in an earthy bed;
> My dust would hear her and beat,
>   Had I lain for a century dead;
> Would start and tremble under her feet,
>   And blossom in purple and red.

It is this promise that the end of the poem fulfils. His earlier vow to 'bury all this dead body of hate' is given ironic fulfilment after the vow is broken; in part II of the poem, in his madness he believes himself buried. He is indeed buried in a Death-in-Life, in a prison of self, with a 'heart of stone', not a 'heart of fire'. In part III he has risen at the call of Maud from this buried life, to seek her 'who tarries for him', where flames 'the blood-red blossom of war'.

It will be seen from this very brief discussion that symbols are used as main elements in the dramatic structure; symbolism is not used simply as lyrical mode, but functions throughout as integral to the total dramatic pattern, whose complexity is fully revealed only by following the patterns of symbol – flower, gem, colour symbols, etc. There is not space here to illustrate at all fully how these operate in the structure; a number of recent critics, notably E. D. H. Johnson and J. H. Buckley, have dealt very ably with the subject, this being an area in which modern criticism is at its best. It might finally be noted, however, that what may be taken to be external action also operates primarily as symbol in *Maud*. The duel is much less important as a physical event that brings a train of physical consequences than as a sudden irruption of hate and of the law of the wood; the 'burial' of the hero in part II is not important as an actual physical incarceration, but as the death-in-life and passive despair produced by the defeat of love; and the departure in part III is not important as a physical departure to help fight the Crimean War, but as the seeking of life-in-death through love.

Given this highly original conception of a 'monodrama', entirely internal in action, Tennyson was bound to seek a highly original mode of presentation. He abandons the formal structure of conventional drama, with its five or three acts and its scenes, and uses instead a succession of what his son Hallam calls 'cantos', which were later divided into the asymmetrical three 'parts' of the final text. The divisions merely emphasize the two main discontinuities in the psychological action which were already there. The final text is a rather bewildering maze of numerals. There are twenty-eight cantos, varying in length from nine lines to over a hundred; the longer ones are sub-divided into as many as nineteen numbered stanzas or thirteen numbered sections which again vary from single couplets to as many as thirty-five lines. The careful numbering is clearly designed to emphasize degrees of discontinuity and of discreteness. To some extent we can recognize in the cantos the equivalent of 'scenes'; each carries through a piece of 'action' belonging to a time or an occasion distinct from the ones before and after. Even when times are not specified, as they often are not, it is as if the shutters of the hero's mind have closed and re-opened to give us a new view of it. In the interval, his mind will have changed its mood, shifted to a new set of thoughts, been stirred by a new set of circumstances or by a new memory. These 'scenes', of varied tempo and length, dissolving and emerging in succession with something like the fluidity of the cinema, make up the units of the drama.

Within the 'scenes' the sub-sections give us what corresponds to the shifting tempo and tone of action on the stage. In the sixth canto of part I, for example, the emotion at the start moves quickly towards joy. In the third section the movement is checked and swings towards the suspicion and doubt in section four. Section five gently insinuates hope again, six moves strongly and vigorously towards hate, which reaches a staccato climax in section seven. This seems to produce a reaction, and in the last three sections the rush of hate slows and stops, and the canto ends with a quiet movement of hope. The sections constantly shift in velocity, in tonality, in mood. Here it is easy to see a sort of analogy with stage drama.

But though this is the general pattern, it is not applicable to all the cantos. In the mad scene of part II each section is as distinct as cantos are elsewhere, presumably to convey the extra disjointedness of complete insanity, in which case it may correspond to the disconnected dialogue and abrupt unrelated action in conventional mad scenes. But many of the cantos are in stanzaic form, and here analogy with ordinary drama breaks down. The stanzaic cantos do, however, suggest another formal analogy to supplement that of conventional stage drama, which will perhaps help us to understand better the structure of *Maud*. This analogy is also the one suggested by a careful look at the actual verse medium or media Tennyson uses.

The poem has often been described as made up of lyrics. The term 'lyric' is broad and vague enough to cover almost any kind of verse, particularly any verse which is rhymed and which is the utterance of a single speaker, as is the case throughout *Maud*. Moreover, the boundaries of the genre of lyric had been stretched by the Romantic poets to include or blend with forms previously separate, as we have already suggested. Browning, for example, puts into his volume of 'Dramatic Lyrics' not only the songs called *Cavalier Tunes*, and the song-like *Through the Metidja*, but dramatic monologues like *My Last Duchess* and *Soliloquy of the Spanish Cloister*, and narratives like *Incident of the French Camp* and *The Pied Piper of Hamelin*. Many of these poems were later re-grouped and became 'Dramatic Romances', but, as De Vane rightly comments, 'the logic of Browning's re-assignment is not always apparent'. His final groupings under the title, 'Dramatic Lyrics', seem hardly more comprehensible than the original. The only principles derivable from the title and the groupings seem to be: that songs or pure lyrics in the volume express the situation and feelings, not of the author, but of the 'dramatic' imagined characters, and that the more purely dramatic pieces, monologue or narrative, are 'lyric' in form – that is, use stanzaic or other rhymed verse. If these are indeed Browning's principles, they could also be said to apply to *Maud*. But this does not get us very far, as it does not get us far to conclude that *Cavalier Tunes*, *My Last Duchess*, and *The Pied Piper* are all rhymed and all 'objective'. To give so broad a sense of 'lyric' is nugatory.

The cantos of *Maud* are of course concerned with a single theme and related into a single structure, which differentiates them from the contents of Browning's volume; but this structure derives from and bears on their quality, not as lyric, but as drama. If we detach cantos from their context to inspect the poetical mode of each, we soon become aware that they exhibit a large range of kinds. At one extreme we have verse so free in its movement, so direct in its syntax, so slightly stylized in its diction, and so unobtrusively rhymed, as to give the effect of normal dramatic verse. This is especially evident in the mad scenes. At the other extreme are verses in pure lyric stanza form, highly stylized in syntax and diction, completely song-like and lyrically self-contained, like 'Go not, happy day' (I. xvii) and the familiar 'Come into the garden, Maud' (I. xxii).

Between these two extremes of something like pure dramatic and pure lyric form lies a whole spectrum of gradations. The free lyrics, like the triumphant 'I have led her home, my love, my only friend' (I. xviii) and the despairing 'O that 'twere possible' (II. iv) have a quality close to the purely lyrical, the latter modulating in many of its sections into formal song, but they are also contributing to the dramatic movement in a less static way than the pure songs. And passages of dramatic narrative are given varied degrees of lyrical effect by control of diction, syntax, and rhyme, as a comparison of, say, 'A voice by the cedar tree' (I. v. i), 'I was walking a mile' (I. ix) and 'So now I have sworn to bury' (I. xix. x) will demonstrate.

The analogy that suggests itself to anyone familiar with seventeenth- and early eighteenth-century music, an analogy not suggested as a model Tennyson had in mind (since he almost certainly did not) but as paralleling closely the sort of structure and the sort of effect *Maud* has when read aloud, is that of the *opera seria*. Here the dramatic narrative is carried forward by *recitativo*, which can be purely dramatic, or almost so, when it is *secco*, but which can be modified by varied degrees of accompaniment and of formalizing, moving into *ariosi* and into highly formal *aria* at certain points in the action. There is in this sort of opera the same sort of spectrum between extremes, and the same sort of facility in modulating from dramatic to lyric. The fundamental differences are of course in the verbal dominance in poetry, the musical in opera, and in the fact that *Maud* is a monodrama.

The versification of *Maud* is immensely skilled. Most of the poem is in a flexible line that moves at need from a three-beat to a four-beat measure, with occasional expansions and retardations to five beats, or with abrupt staccato stops through the insertion of a two-beat line. The units are verse paragraphs in which line lengths and rhyme schemes are matched to the syntax; it is almost impossible to find two identical rhyme schemes in any of the non-stanzaic sections.

The opening and the close of the poem are in stanzaic form – the first canto is in fact the longest stanzaic passage in the poem. Stanzas are clearly not confined to *arias*, since the effect of this canto is dominantly dramatic, rather than lyric. This is partly because of the nature of the stanza chosen, a loose alternate hexameter quatrain, and partly because the syntax is dramatic, not lyric. The long line allows great choice of phrasing and the development of large rhetorical patterns, rather like those Tennyson developed in the fifteener lines of *Locksley Hall*. And the rhetoric is dramatic. The hexameter line is continued through the first four cantos, the longest sequence of regular form in the poem. The fifth canto shifts the mode, with powerful effect, to the lyrical, in 'A voice by the cedar tree'.

The concluding Part III is again regular, using throughout five-beat lines, though not in stanzas. The large structure thus bears some resemblance to that of *The Lotos-Eaters* which we examined earlier, in which a regular opening moved into free choric forms and then to a regular close in a new metre. So here, the opening hexameters establish a tempo and an emotional tone, which continue to beat and echo through the fluctuations and dramatic contrasts which follow. The resolution brings a new pulse, a new kind of ordered movement, and a new emotional tone. In *Maud* the opening pulse and energy is that of hate, the closing one is of love.

Maud, then, is not only a virtuoso poetic performance, but a most radical experiment in drama, where a dramatic action having a beginning, a middle, and an end, embodying the classical patterns of conflict, irony, *peripeteia*, and final resolution, is made entirely internal and psychological, and in which the form abandons the external pattern and proportion of conventional drama to use a complex variety of verse forms organized into 'movements', and into scenes within the movements. Narrative, dramatic, and lyric elements are fused or modulated into each other by techniques similar to those of *opera seria*, with its varied forms of *recitative* and *arias*. The theme of the whole is self-contained in that the resolution is implicit in the opening situation, both being fundamentally internal; it is the final state of mind that is implicit in the first.

The form of *In Memoriam* has some affinity with that of *Maud*, in that it uses 'cantos' or sections of limited length, nominally 'lyrical' but moving from narrative to dramatic to lyric, in a larger structure that is at least partly dramatic. Like other elegies, it has its origin in personal experience, and draws upon it, but the experience is itself a universal one, and the elegy works it into a formal pattern that objectifies and dramatizes it. Consequently, the 'I' of the poem is never simply Tennyson: it is Everyman facing the enigma of death, sorrow, and suffering, and of a cosmic order in which these jarring elements are found. It is accordingly a mistake to keep referring the details of the poem to details in Tennyson's own life, as if the poem were a personal diary, or to call the chronology of the poem, as indicated by the recurring Christmas and anniversary cantos, an 'artificial' one because it does not correspond to the actual long time of its composition. The chronology is not transferred from the sequence of personal experience, but is an essential part of the formal structure.

That structure is so original and so complex as to be entirely *sui generis*, although it draws, like all Tennyson's experiments, upon traditions of genre. The basic method of composition, in cantos or sections made up of quatrains, and the very close texture of the writing in the cantos, makes the task of grasping the complete structure very difficult without long and close study, and it is small wonder that readers become fascinated by individual cantos or by short sequences, which they contemplate out of the context of the whole. What particularly gets obscured is the fact that this is an elegy, in memory of Arthur Hallam, and that the core of its structure is the traditional classical elegiac form. This is a genre which has had a very long life in Western literatures. It pays tribute to the dead person in whose honour it is written in two ways: as a work of art, or artifact, and as an expression of grief and love. As a work of art, it is like a sculpture or a funeral monument, or a funeral ode or musical anthem, a carefully wrought offering rendering public honour. As an expression of grief and love, it is a public avowal of the dead man's worth: 'by the measure of my grief', the poet writes, 'I leave thy greatness to be guessed'. The elegy thus combines a highly formal aspect and an emotional one, both designed to honour the subject.

It is perhaps unfortunate that the elegies with which English readers are most familiar, Milton's *Lycidas* and Shelley's *Adonais*, do not achieve a balance between these aspects. In both these poems, the reader's attention is concentrated on the formal beauty and on the author rather than on the subject: we certainly read *Lycidas* for what it tells us about Milton, not for what makes King worthy of honour; Milton's *Epitaphium Damonis*, honouring his friend Diodati, is a more balanced work. Furthermore, now that the formal elegy is completely out of fashion, it is difficult for the modern reader to understand the way in which the formal conventions and obvious artificialities, particularly of the pastoral mode, can convey real depth of feeling. Yet, as we have noted, the formal elegy has had a long literary life, which suggests that it has a true correspondence with the realities of human experience. This becomes evident if we consider what may be called the thematic pattern of the convention. This opens with a statement of the subject, 'Weep for him, for he is dead', and expresses the deep sense of mourning shared by the whole of Nature, or calls on Nature to mourn. Then comes a questioning raised by the loss – why did this death have to happen? Recollections of the past shared by the poet with his dead friend begin to bring comfort, which changes to exaltation with the thought of the friend's apotheosis and continuing life, and the poem ends with the final turning away from sorrow back to the world. This pattern is recognizable as a formalized and condensed version of the actual pattern of emotion after a bereavement, so that in its conventional shape the pastoral elegy simplifies and condenses the actual shape of human experience, from wild questioning grief to acceptance. By imposing an aesthetic pattern it gives the emotion relief and also meaning, as does formal tragedy.

And this pattern is the basic thematic pattern of *In Memoriam*, as Tennyson reminds us at certain points in the poem by deliberate echoes of the pastoral mode. But for Tennyson, and for his age, some of the traditions of the formal elegy were no longer valid. As we have seen, he is seldom willing to write a strictly conventional poem; he will use the power of convention and tradition, but is fully aware that conventions expressive for one age are dead for another. As he has the poet say in *The Epic*, 'A truth looks freshest in the fashion of the day . . . nature brings not back the mastodon . . . and why should any man Remodel models?' Specifically, his view of nature makes the conventional call to Nature to mourn an empty one; and the questioning of order and justice raised by the death of Hallam goes far beyond the conventional. Nor could he give to the questioning the conventional answers; none of the earlier modes of theodicy, either theological or philosophical, seem to him persuasive.

In short, the emotional pattern is still valid and universal, but not the conventional pattern of thought and ideas; the questions raised by grief and the kind of answers that can be offered are not permanently valid from age to age. The questions and answers are now more complex, the answers more hesitant and speculative; they cannot be rendered in a brief formula, so the condensation of the classical elegy must be abandoned for something on a much larger scale, for something allowing dramatic movements of conflict, elaboration of perplexities, fears, hopes, intimations, speculations, and affirmations. The general shape which formalizes and releases the emotions can be retained, but not within the conventional limits or the conventional short time-scale. To extend the time-scale is to bring the movements of emotion closer to the actual, and to explore them in greater detail; it is also, of course, to sacrifice the simple clarity of the traditional form, necessitating an auxiliary principle of structure. This Tennyson provides through a system of internal chronology, counterpointing a rhythm marked by recurring seasons and anniversaries against the basic rhythm of the elegy. The recurrences invite echoes and cross-references, creating movements within the larger movements, and binding parts together in patterns of related themes. The linear pattern of the formal elegy is thus replaced by a highly complex one, in which the clear succession of movements is blurred by overlappings, interfusions, anticipations, reflections and retrospects, by movements set against movements, and so on. Further complications of texture are provided by the extensive use of symbols, many of them recurring, gathering meaning or modulations of meaning as they reappear in varied contexts, and further binding parts tightly together into a structure of amazing intricacy. This complexity, conveying so strong a sense of the actual complexity of human emotion and thought, is the very essence of the poem; yet under it all the broad shape from grief to reconciliation is still discernible and powerfully working.

The virtuosity with which Tennyson uses the simple-looking octosyllabic quatrain, with its invariable *abba* rhyme scheme, is apparent to every reader. Cantos vary from twelve lines to ten times that length; some quatrains are totally stopped, isolated like inscriptions, elsewhere five will flow freely in a single sustained sentence. Sometimes successive cantos will be of the same length, three or four or five quatrains, establishing a regular measure, to be completed or given a climax by a longer canto. The diction is throughout relatively simple, but has varied degrees of heightening; it moves from physical description or direct expression of feeling or thought (as in canto VII) to frequent use of personification, apostrophe, and symbol; the syntax ranges from the almost flatly direct to the fully rhetorical (as in canto XI). His variations of tonality, of metrical phrasing, of quantitative pattern, and of syntactic structure are so infinitely inventive that to read the poem aloud as it should be read is to be aware that patterns are only repeated at those particular points where he wants an echo or reminiscence. Elsewhere one gets the impression that no two lines, let alone quatrains, are alike; there seem to be no favourite tonal or metrical devices recurring frequently to his ear. An examination of a few sample lines suggests that one of the sources of this unusual variety is Tennyson's subordination of accent and stress; the verse is for the most part very lightly accented, so that quantity or length of syllable plays a much larger part in the phrasing than accent. This seems to be the main technical explanation of why the lines in *In Memoriam* never have the kind of movement and tempo normally characteristic of octosyllabics. Indeed, many readers of *In Memoriam* are not conscious that it has the same octosyllabic line as Milton's *L'Allegro*, Swift's *Beasts' Confession*, Prior's *Alma*, Coleridge's *Christabel*, Scott's *The Lady of the Lake* and Burns' *Tam O'Shanter*. The swift pace and vigorous thrust which in these examples seem natural to the metre are totally absent from Tennyson's lines, which often move at a pace which suggests the reflective tempo of the decasyllabic line. It is the accents, and especially their regular distribution, which normally give octosyllabics such a brisk movement. Tennyson lightens the accents and, where he distributes them evenly, either reduces their impact by his quantitative pattern, or slows the line by monosyllables. Almost any line in the poem can provide an example of his interesting techniques; here are some chosen virtually at random: 'Dost thou look back on what hath been' (LXIV) illustrates the light accent, use of monosyllables, and of quantity; 'Tonight the winds begin to rise' (XV) is very complex; the vowels within the line make their own *abba* pattern, 'night', 'winds', 'gin', 'rise', with the effect of double rhyme, 'Tonight', 'to rise', 'the winds', 'begin', and the length of the syllable 'winds', followed by the labial of 'begin', creates a slight pause at the centre. 'On the bald street breaks the blank day' (VII) is strongly and unusually accented, so that it explodes at the end of the section, but the accents are neither normal in number nor position: only the two articles 'the' are entirely without accent, and the pattern is essentially - ◡ - - / - ◡ - -, all in monosyllables, with the stresses stronger, with *b b d*, in the second half. 'When on my bed the moonlight falls' (LXVII) starts very lightly in the first half, then is retarded by the three syllables, all long, at the end of the line.

The tempo is not uniform; like the tonality, it is constantly changing, sometimes within the quatrain, often within the canto. Some lines do in fact move as rapidly as one expects from octo-syllabics, but not through the thrust of accent: 'A happy lover who has come To look on her that loves him well' (VIII) is very lightly accented, and moves with a light grace and delicacy, punctuated by the alliterated *l*s; note that the second line, with its monosyllables, slightly slows the pace, which is further retarded through the rest of the canto. Strong accents, where they occur, are created by the initial consonants, and are used as in music for a strong and resonant 'attack', as distinguished from a smooth *legato*; they are found in passages of strong emotion or of resonant affirmation. There is skilful modulation, to take a single example, in the last quatrain of canto LXXXVI:

> From belt to belt of crimson seas
> On leagues of odour streaming far,
> To where in yonder orient star
> A hundred spirits whisper 'Peace.'

Here the accented resonance of the first line smooths into slow *legato* in the second line, and slows and hushes to the final word.

The poem is so packed with this sort of detailed artistry that one is tempted to pursue it endlessly, but it is always necessary to return to the work as a whole to which all this minute beauty is contributory. A volume would not exhaust the riches of detail, nor reveal all the poetic relation of part to part, of the intricate control of tone and tempo in something like musical movements, the effects Tennyson produces by changes in diction, syntax, and metrical structure in developing these movements in relation to the whole. But we must never forget the nature of that whole as a great elegy. The fundamental theme of all elegies in the traditional mode is the triumph of love over death, fear and doubt. The most familiar lines in *In Memoriam*, hackneyed by repetition and by unthinking and insensitive quotation, assert the theme: ''Tis better to have loved and lost Than never to have loved at all' – a statement of the supreme value of love, which outweighs the sorrow and doubts that accompany love and the death of the beloved. The sorrow and the doubts are indeed a tribute to love. This theme, developed in such detail and with such sincerity, makes *In Memoriam* the greatest elegy in English literature. No other elegy pays so impressive a tribute to its subject, or gives us so full and lively a portrait. Hallam's charm, his quick intelligence, his philosophical mind, the gaiety of his companionship, the affection he inspired in his friends, all come home to us with vividness and power. The force of Tennyson's love for him, the moving force of the poem, is not an interesting peculiarity of the poet's character which he wishes to explore; it is a great and moving tribute to a unique personality whose loss was deeply felt by all who knew him, and whose finest and most permanent memorial is this poem.

The *Idylls of the King*, Tennyson's longest poem, also exhibits a highly complex and very experimental structure. Its composition extended over an even longer period than that of *In Memoriam*: the first part of it published, *Morte d'Arthur*, (later incorporated into *The Passing of Arthur*), appeared in 1842; the last, *Balin and Balan*, in 1885. The first use of the title, *Idylls of the King*, was in 1859, for a small volume containing four idylls: *Enid*, (later expanded and divided into *The Marriage of Geraint* and *Geraint and Enid*), *Nimuë*, (later revised and re-named *Merlin and Vivien*), *Elaine*, and *Guinevere*. The first two had been privately printed in 1857 as *Enid and Nimuë: The True and the False*, and all four appeared first in a private trial edition in 1859 as *The True and the False: Four Idylls of the King*.

Ten years later, in December 1869, under the title *The Holy Grail and Other Poems* appeared *The Coming of Arthur*, *The Holy Grail*, *Pelleas and Ettarre* and *The passing of Arthur*. *The Last Tournament* was published in the *Contemporary Review* in December 1871, then in a volume with *Gareth and Lynette* in October 1872. In the next year *Geraint and Enid* was divided and the whole poem, except for *Balin and Balan*, was printed together in *Works* with a new epilogue. *Balin and Balan*, although written at this period (1872–4), was not published until 1885.

Superficially, a knowledge of the piecemeal publication, and the recognition of obvious differences in treatment among the idylls, create a presumption that here is merely a loose collection of independent narratives, yoked by their common source of theme in the Arthurian material, but having little organic unity as a single poem. This indeed was the judgement of many critics for many years, and reinforced the opinion that Tennyson had no powers of large construction. Once this opinion is accepted, there is little inclination to read his longer works from beginning to end as single poems: the 'best bits' are anthologized, the rest forgotten, and total structure is no longer looked for on the confident assumption that it is not there. This has often been the fate of *In Memoriam* and of the *Idylls*. To some extent, as we have seen, this is the effect of a failure to recognize the unorthodox nature of Tennyson's experimental structure. Since there are twelve idylls, it is easy to assume a connection with the epic, and to judge the poem by the 'rules' or conventions of the traditional epic, coming to the natural conclusion that Tennyson wished to write an epic but was not equal to the task. Or again, since Tennyson, particularly in *The Passing of Arthur*, follows Malory at times very closely, sometimes indeed virtually making a blank verse paraphrase, there is a tendency to think that this is his purpose, and consequently to object to departures from Malory's authorized version. Critics like Carlyle, in the poet's own time, objected that the poem was 'escape', mere pretty 'art for art's sake', not sufficiently connected with the real problems of nineteenth-century England; critics in the early twentieth century have found it, on the contrary, too Victorian. These varied attitudes indicate confusion about the poet's aims and the poem's nature and structure. In the last twenty years, thanks partly to the perspective time brings, critics have come to recognize what the poem is, and it is now receiving full attention as Tennyson's most ambitious, and perhaps greatest, work.

There can be little doubt that the poem has a total structure, and that it is designed. His son Hallam tells us that before 1840 his father's choice of form had wavered between epic and drama. Tennyson himself speaks of his intention, before 1842, to write an epic: 'I had it all in my mind', he says, '. . . But then I thought that a small vessel, built on fine lines, is likely to float further down the stream of Time than a big raft'. His image is an interesting one, in view of the fact that to those who see the final work as a loosely tied collection of separate and independent narratives, the raft is the more appropriate figure. The small vessel 'built on fine lines' clearly indicates that the alternative structure Tennyson chose, in abandoning the epic, appears to him as a unity, smaller but more refined and sophisticated in design. According to his son Hallam, by 1855 Tennyson had 'determined upon the final shape of the poem'. But Hallam further tells us, in connection with the publication of the *Four Idylls* in 1859, that his father 'had carried a more or less perfected scheme . . . in his head over thirty years'. In 1862 Tennyson writes, 'I have thought about it, and arranged all the intervening Idylls', but completion and publication were delayed by his fears of failure and his doubts of the public reception. In 1873, when all but *Balin and Balan* had been published, Tennyson insisted to R. H. Hutton that he 'must have two more Idylls at the least to make *Vivien* come later into the Poem, as it comes in far too soon as it stands'. In that year he divided *Geraint and Enid* into two idylls, and in 1885 produced *Balin and Balan* for insertion between the *Geraint and Enid* idylls and *Vivien*, the *Merlin and Vivien* thus becoming the sixth idyll. Before 1873 it had been the fourth.

What can we plausibly infer from these pieces of external evidence? If Hallam is right in saying that Tennyson had carried 'a more or less perfected scheme' in his head 'over thirty years' by 1859, it seems evident that the scheme did not include a final decision on the genre, since the period of this 'over thirty years' included the wavering between epic and drama, and having it 'all in his mind' as an epic, then the rejection of epic form for the idylls. The 'scheme', then, since it is represented as staying virtually intact in Tennyson's mind through all the years and the changes in decision as to treatment, must have been one susceptible of each kind of treatment considered. The obvious primary choice the poet must have made as he began to turn over in his mind the vast materials of the Arthurian cycle would be one of subject-matter: clearly one would start with the coming of Arthur and end with his passing, but what in between? This is the point at which a 'scheme' becomes necessary, whether the chosen incidents are to be used in an epic or in a drama. Along with the selection of the narrative elements must have come a sense of their order in a sequence, subject of course to later rearrangement, but forming a pattern of development or movement according to some clear principle. This is indicated by the mention of the 'final shape' determined by 1855, and of having 'arranged all the intervening *Idylls*' by 1862; 'final shape' suggests previous tentative shapes, and it is then clear that the 'intervening idylls', that is, those required to complete the scheme, have now been given their final place. The decision to insert further idylls before the *Vivien* is expressed in terms of a very clear view of the whole structure and the place in it *Vivien* must have. All this early planning can be seen as related to the selection and conduct of the narrative elements.

But other modes of planning accompany and to some extent shape these decisions. For Tennyson the main attraction of the Arthurian stories was not the romance of high adventure, nor a romantic nostalgia for the past, though these are elements to which he also responds as a poet. From the first, when as a boy he read Malory, Arthur had represented for him an ideal for man's imitation, and the stories of Arthur's exploits, his victories and defeat and passing, represented, as he later put it 'the unending war of humanity in all ages, – the world-wide war of sense and soul . . .' His approach to the Arthurian material had always had in it an 'allegorical drift', or, as he later said, 'perhaps rather a parabolic drift'. He had never intended merely to re-tell old stories, or to 'remodel models'. The attraction of the story of Arthur was not simply that it was romantic, picturesque, and dramatic; it also held meanings of universal significance for man and society. And universal meanings are also contemporary; Arthur's story had things to say to Tennyson's own age, as to all ages. His substitution of 'parabolic' for 'allegorical' reveals something of how his conception developed. Allegory is not the same thing as parable; in allegory there is usually a direct and simple correspondence between the thing allegorized and its representation in the allegory, so that in *Pilgrim's Progress*, for example, the helpful character Interpreter can point out to the reader the precise and specific meaning of allegorical characters or incidents. Parable is much less specific and consequently much broader and more flexible in its meanings. Tennyson's early notes, written about 1833, show that at first he was thinking in terms of very specific allegory: 'K.A. Religious Faith . . . Two Guineveres. The first prim. Christianity. 2d Roman Catholicism . . . Modred, the sceptical understanding . . . Merlin Emrys, the enchanter, Science . . . Excalibur, war . . . The Round Table: liberal institutions . . .'. He must soon have recognized that the more specific an allegory is, the more difficult it becomes to give it a universal meaning, and that detailed allegory with a constant simple equivalence leads the reader into a process of translation from allegorical into literal terms, leaving him with a literal and limited 'message' instead of a poem. Further, the allegorist is forced, in simple allegory, into development shaped by the literal matter he is allegorizing. Parable gives him a much greater range of freedom; as Tennyson says elsewhere, 'liberal applications lie In Art like Nature', and the meaning of a parable is not soon exhausted. As he also says, 'the thought within the image is much more than any one interpretation . . . ; poetry is like shot-silk with many glancing colours'.

The shot-silk image is a particularly happy one for the *Idylls*. The parable operates at three levels: 'The whole', Tennyson said, 'is the dream of man coming into practical life and ruined by one sin. Birth is a mystery and death is a mystery, and in the midst lies the tableland of life, and its struggles and performances. It is not the history of one man or of one generation but of a whole cycle of generations . . . I intended Arthur to represent the Ideal Soul of Man coming into contact with the warring elements of the flesh'. Tennyson here puts the emphasis on the most universal level of meaning, the application to 'a whole cycle of generations', but the universal contains the particular, and the meaning has application also to one generation, or one society, and also to the single human life. Arthur is the soul of any man coming into this world, struggling for the true and the good, and passing from the world; he is also the soul of any society or social organism, the animating principles and ideals on which the life of a society depend; and he is the soul of Mankind. The Round Table is the symbol of the order, individual, social, human, created by these ideals and values; as an 'image of the mighty world', it is a symbol of the cosmos created by spirit, of the microcosmos of individual man, of society or nation, of cycles of societies and nations, which, Tennyson recognizes, must be shaped and animated by various manifestations of the same eternal and unchanging spirit. The tragic collapse of Arthur's world shows the return to chaos and disorder in the life of individual, society, or the whole of humanity when the spirit which animates all, and the spiritual values that serve as principles of order, are rejected or overcome. The three levels, individual, social, and universal, are not so tightly related as to be readily allegorized simultaneously: their relation to each other is essentially a metaphoric one, based on the ancient metaphors of man as a microcosm, and of the body politic. Consequently, while it is easy to see the primary theme of 'Soul at war with Sense' throughout in terms of all three levels, and to recognize violent figures of evil like Earl Doorm, or sinister undercover workers of evil like Modred as representing either forces within the individual or forces within a society, or even cosmic forces of evil, attempts to interpret all characters and all action in terms of the three levels run into insuperable difficulties. Some early critics, for example, tried to work out a complete allegory at the first level by making each member of Arthur's court represent some faculty or quality in individual man. Merlin was to be Reason, Lancelot Imagination, Vivien Sensuality, and so on. The attempt failed, and at best served in only the most obvious general application. It did illustrate Tennyson's point, that his method is not strictly allegorical, but parabolic. Many of the idylls defy any simple allegorical approach. In some, the reader's attention is directed naturally towards thinking of Arthur's kingdom as a social structure, and emblem of all social structures, rather than as an emblem of individual man. The shot-silk suggests that this was Tennyson's intention: his weaving of the three levels of meaning, like three colours, shows dominantly now this, now that level.

The very general pattern of meaning stands out quite clearly as the reader contemplates the poem as a whole, with his primary attention focused by the first and last 'coming and passing' idylls on Arthur and his cosmos that is built and then destroyed. But the pattern is by no means clear and dominant in the intervening idylls. It rather flashes into view for varied lengths of time and with varied degrees of force within contexts that often seem to offer other patterns. The essentials of the main theme are given in five of the idylls: *The Coming of Arthur, Merlin and Vivien, The Holy Grail, The Last Tournament,* and *The Passing of Arthur.* Important additions and elaborations of it are included in other idylls: the first 467 lines of *Gareth and Lynette*, the concluding part of *Geraint and Enid*, the implications of the story of *Pelleas and Ettarre*, and much of *Guinevere*. But these also develop other themes with something like a collateral relation to the main one, and some of the idylls, notably *The Marriage of Geraint*, *Balin and Balan*, and *Lancelot and Elaine*, are built on strong secondary themes. These themes become parables in themselves, embodying whole meanings which can be related to the whole meaning of the main parable. There are also parables within parables, like the victories of Gareth over Time and Death in the persons of the knights Morning-Star, Noonday Sun, Evening, Night and Death; Phosphorus, Meridies, Hesperus, Nox and Mors, and his discovery within the skull of Death of 'the bright face of a blooming boy'. *The Holy Grail* is indeed a collection of parables that form one parable, since each knight has a different experience in the quest, and each experience has its own meaning.

Balin and Balan, the last written of the idylls and one of the most original, with its strong suggestion of individual man at war with himself, the conflict being not so simply 'Soul at war with Sense', but rather love and loyalty to order at war with the violent passions of anger and fierce hatred, creates its own powerful and almost self-contained parable. It suddenly illuminates elements in the main theme briefly introduced in earlier idylls through characters like Limours, Edyrn, and Earl Doorm. Positive forces of brutality, violence and anarchy, hitherto presented as external, now appear also parabolically as internal: the enemy is within as well as without.

The story of Lancelot and Guinevere is, apart from that of Arthur, the most continuously developed; their guilty love and its effects are felt very early in *The Marriage of Geraint*. Doubts of Guinevere's purity provide in various ways motives for action in that idyll, in *Balin and Balan*, in *Merlin and Vivien*, and in *Pelleas and Ettarre*. Lancelot himself is frequently introduced into the action of the idylls, and we are kept aware of the development of his tragic career almost as steadily as of Arthur's, giving a sense of two interwoven main narrative threads. But the Lancelot–Guinevere story is essentially different in kind from Arthur's. It does not strike us as fundamentally symbolic or allegorical. We look for symbolic or allegorical meaning in the marriage of Arthur and Guinevere, and are encouraged to do so by lines in the poem (particularly lines 76–93 in *The Coming of Arthur*). Their union is the union of Soul and Body whereby the Spirit can 'mix itself with life', and the Idea can be actualized; the union of eternal and temporal. But we seek no such meanings, nor are they suggested, for the love of Lancelot and Guinevere. Yet we recognize that what Tennyson said about the meaning of the whole poem, that it is 'the dream of man coming into practical life and ruined by one sin', is also a description of the career of Lancelot. But in Lancelot's case, the sin is his, and is deliberate and voluntary: he sees the higher and knowingly chooses the lower. Guinevere's sin is less deliberate; she comes only at the end to recognize the value of what she has rejected and betrayed. The two provide, at the human level, *exempla* of the main theme, so that the characters, and particularly Guinevere, serve a double function, as elements in the main parabolic pattern and as principals in a narrative at a different level.

The blending of allegorical and realistic modes in a single work goes back at least as far as Bunyan's *Pilgrim's Progress*; the mixture obviously creates no difficulty for the unsophisticated reader, and there seems to be no reason why it should for the sophisticated. The realistic narratives provide illustrations or *exempla* of the more abstract or universal theme presented in allegory; the allegory presents a general or universal comment on the significance of the realistic particular narrative. In *Merlin and Vivien* Tennyson indeed fuses the two modes; the psychology of Merlin's seduction by Vivien is highly realistic, but the reader is also constantly aware of the abstract meaning of Vivien's victory. The poet does not limit himself in the *Idylls* to the two simple modes, either in characters or in narratives. He establishes a whole series of gradations, and of degrees of fusion of mode. The idyll of *Gareth and Lynette*, for example, has as its core the romance narrative of Gareth's service, which may be taken as an exemplary parable of true knighthood, but is neither primarily realistic nor allegorical. His winning of Lynette is a variant of the taming of the shrew. His dedication to Arthur, and his motives for going to Arthur's court, supplement the allegory or parable of the previous idyll, and his victories over the knights establish a very purely allegorical pattern of their own. *Pelleas and Ettarre*, as a study in disillusionment and destroyed faith, forms a counterbalance to *Gareth and Lynette*, the two characters in each being set in fierce contrast to each other, but the treatment in the later idyll is much simpler than in the earlier, and more given to a presentation of the psychology of despair and disillusionment at something like a realistic level. *Lancelot and Elaine*, in its setting of romantic pastoral, is dominated by a sense of the purely human situation. The poem as a whole thus exhibits a great range of modes, and consequently of styles suitable to each mode. This means, obviously, that it needs a strong structure to bind it together.

The basic structural pattern, and the one undoubtedly present in some form in Tennyson's mind from a very early stage in the composition, is the dramatic movement inherent in the rise and fall of Arthur and his kingdom. We can recognize in the total sequence of the twelve idylls a three-part structure very much like that of a drama in three acts. The first four idylls show generally the triumph of good over evil, the establishing of Arthur's order, the victory of truth over falsehood, of life over death. Arthur is sure of his identity and purpose, and Gareth, dedicated to his service, recognizes Arthur's kingship without question, and knows from the first the meaning and end of his own life. The mood and tone of Gareth's idyll is joyous and confident. The two Geraint idylls modify this tone and mood. Geraint has in him elements of doubt and ferocity which are more disturbing than Lynette's perverse coquettishness, and Enid, seen as a counterpart to Gareth, lacks his strength, although showing similar devotion. Evil becomes more apparent, and less easily overcome, in these two idylls, so that although they too end in happy resolutions and victory, and with a re-establishment of the tone and mood of the opening idylls, the dramatic tension has begun to mount, and to prepare for the second movement.

This opens with a tremendous impact, the grim and violent *Balin and Balan*, followed at once by the sinister triumph of Vivien over Merlin. Merlin's seduction, with all its overtones of Man's first fall, and with its special symbolism of Merlin as Seer and chief builder, Bard and possessor of Wisdom, clearly marks the turning point of the drama. It comes at the centre, the sixth idyll, and henceforth the movement is towards the catastrophe and the coda. The second half of the middle movement, and of the total poem, abruptly shifts tone and style in *Lancelot and Elaine*. Tennyson's orchestration, trumpets and discordant brass in *Balin and Balan*, seductive strings overcoming the brass in *Merlin and Vivien,* dying off to a melancholy, slow, minor theme of defeat, now goes back to the pastoral woodwinds and light strings of the earlier movement. We look back again from death and destruction to the world that was and might still be: Elaine's world is like Gareth's world, certain and serene. The destruction of this world and of Elaine by Lancelot is a human tragedy in itself, full of tragic ironies but also powerful in its reflections and interplay with other themes in the poem. In *Gareth and Lynette* the power of true love and loyal devotion overcame discord and united two lovers; here Elaine's patient fidelity is recognized from the start and fully valued by Lancelot, but can provoke no response but pity. Lancelot has chosen a course he knows to be evil, and clings to it with a perverse deliberate loyalty as strong as Elaine's pure loyalty to him. In the early idylls, Lynette and Geraint undergo changes of heart, Gareth and Enid are steadfast in love; here there can be no change of heart, and Lancelot sadly and knowingly destroys Elaine, not wanting to, but nevertheless choosing to. The Merlin in him still sees and knows, but has been closed in the hollow tower by his Vivien, and made impotent to stir his will. And over the bright world of youth, beauty, faith and love, the Spring world of Gareth, Enid and Elaine, is drawn the pall of sin and death.

The Holy Grail continues this sense of the conflict of two worlds, and also by its structure emphasizes the theme of disintegration. We are no longer aware of a cohesive and coherent court, a Round Table. We are instead hearing a succession of individual adventures of individual knights, each pursuing his own quest of the Grail, a quest in which Arthur does not join, and of which he has not approved. The knights no longer ask the King to assign them a task; all coherence is gone. Each quest and its result has its own meaning, but the meaning of the whole idyll is clearly centred on the collapse of Arthur's authority and the destruction of the Round Table; at the end of the quest Arthur is left 'gazing at a barren board, And a lean Order – scarce return'd a tithe'.

The last movement again opens with an idyll of savage and brutal impact, *Pelleas and Ettarre*; a powerfully ironic, distorted counterpart of the *Gareth and Lynette* story. Pelleas has at the time of his arrival at Arthur's court the youth and eagerness of Gareth, but none of the clarity of spiritual vision. His motivation is secular, to win fame and a beautiful lady; his ideals are a vulgarized version of courtly love, not those of Christian service. Nor is the lady he sets his heart on another Lynette. She is an experienced harlot, contemptuous of Pelleas' puppy-love and sexual amateurism. Pelleas mistakes her scornful rejection for maidenly coquettishness, and when she and Gawain casually betray him, turns half-mad with disillusionment and rebels against Arthur and his order. Here again Tennyson exploits the dramatic contrast between what the world of the Round Table was and what it has become, between the innocence, gaiety, and sureness of Gareth's world, and the corruption, feverish sensuality, and suspicion of Pelleas'. The style and matter, penetrated with a harsh cynicism, reinforce the contrast. The next idyll continues the pattern. The knights no longer wage war on evil, nor train to fit themselves for that war: *The Last Tournament* is a mere contest for prizes, a contest in which the most skilful, not the worthiest, wins by cheating as much as by skill. The prize is the ruby necklace called the jewels of dead innocence; the winner is Tristram, who rejects all that Arthur stands for. Lancelot presides over the competition, sees the rules broken, and 'spake not'. This is the end of the Round Table, the last meeting together of the knights before they meet as opponents in the last destructive civil war. The tournament is an empty form, a shell of ritual and external show from which all meaning and spirit have departed, and the whole idyll is penetrated with deeper and deeper irony.

Guinevere begins the coda with a change of tone. The bitter irony of the two preceding idylls is replaced by a sad, elegiac sense of loss, of waste, of too late recognition. This tone appears most powerfully in Guinevere's repentance, as she sees, with newly opened eyes, the worth of what she has brought to ruin. The final idyll, *The Passing of Arthur*, moves back to the high symbolic style of the opening, and in Arthur's last speech, in the taking up of his sword Excalibur by the arm 'clothed in white samite, mystic, wonderful', and in his vanishing into the dawn, greeted by the faint sounds heard by Sir Bedivere, 'as if some fair city were one voice Around a king returning from his wars', the whole drama is placed in a cosmic and eternal perspective. Emotion is calmed, then moved in the final lines to hope, as 'the new sun rose bringing the new year'.

The total structure follows closely the thematic rhythm of drama, and to read the poem as a continuous whole is to be aware of the power of its dramatic pattern, to feel terror and pity, and final acceptance of tragic loss. It will already be apparent, however, that the twelve-part structure is by no means simply ordered. The 'three-act' pattern, with four idylls to each 'act' is there indeed, but it is by no means the only pattern. Other rhythms are created by the ironic linkages we have noted, by shifts of tone, of emotional impact, and of tempo. The wide range of choice open to Tennyson through the use of the loosely defined 'idyll' form allows him to create a dramatic parable of enormous variety, richness, and complexity, while retaining the strong and relatively simple shape of tragedy.

CHAPTER 5

'Meanings ambushed':
The oblique use of language

THE young poet, intoxicated by the seemingly inexhaustible resources of language, rejoicing in its rich variety, is inclined to believe that there is nothing he cannot make it do – it seems a perfectly plastic and flexible medium. For the purposes of his poetry at the youthful stage, he is probably right; experience has not yet touched him deeply, he is all eye and ear, excited by what Browning calls 'the very superficial taste of things', and his poetry tries to capture in brilliant, sharp exactness the look of the brave new world about him, and to convey the excitement of it. Wordsworth's description of this stage in the poet's career is unsurpassed, and clearly is entirely typical. Besides Wordsworth's 'influence of natural objects', both Keats and Tennyson came under the influence of books, and added to the excitement of the world of Nature that of the world of literature. At this stage, the poet is close to living the life the young Keats sighed for, a 'life of sensation' rather than one of thought. But experience of life accumulates, 'shades of the prison-house' of the world modify the bright vision, the 'still, sad music of humanity' adds its solemn notes to the joyous strains, and the poet finds himself with thoughts and feelings no longer easily or directly communicable in language. 'Thoughts that do often lie too deep for tears' also lie too deep to be spread out on a surface of language.

If one wished to add to the ingenious interpretations of *The Lady of Shalott*, it would be easy to see its allegory as that of young poetry, seeing the outer world brilliantly enhanced in the mirror but reduced to a two-dimensional surface, and catching its superficial beauty in the two-dimensional tapestry. This young poetry has, indeed, 'a lovely face', but it is destroyed by life and by those other dimensions of which the young poet becomes aware – its web floats wide as the spell is broken. Never again can the young poet see the world in simply sensuous terms, as a picture: the curse of the prison-house, of the human condition, is unavoidable and irreversible. Death and suffering bring maturity to Wordsworth, to Keats, to Tennyson, to all young poets and to all the young who are not abnormally insensitive.

And with maturity comes the problem for the young poet of how to express the inexpressible. Many years ago E. M. W. Tillyard wrote a book about poetry, distinguishing two sorts, direct and oblique. The distinction is a useful one if it is not taken too seriously, like the other common critical distinction which sets apart 'poetry of statement' from other poetry. It is in fact very difficult to define 'direct' or 'statement' in relation to the use of language, even in prose, and highly doubtful whether any line of real poetry is 'direct' or a 'statement'. Dr Johnson's famous parody of the ballad,

> I put my hat upon my head
>   And walked into the Strand,
> And there I met another man,
>   Whose hat was in his hand,

is as 'direct' a 'statement' as one could find, but the 'statement' of the facts of Johnson's walk is not what the verse is about: it contains, rather, a 'statement' of Johnson's opinion of ballads. Again, stripped of its familiar context, Shakespeare's 'Full fathom five thy father lies', makes a 'direct statement': 'Your father is lying in at least thirty feet of water'. These examples, then, must be taken as 'oblique', since they are not designed primarily to make a direct statement. But virtually no poetry seems so designed; all poetry seems to function at least partly by indirection. In fact, nearly all language means more than it seems to say, except in purely technical uses like recipes for cooking or mechanics' handbooks. But there is clearly a large range of degrees of indirection: some poetry is more 'oblique' than others, so that some seems to function almost entirely by indirection.

We have seen, for example, that in his revision of poems for the 1842 volume, Tennyson largely replaced description of a primarily pictorial intention by description which was primarily symbolic. The original descriptions were not in fact *solely* topographical or pictorial, their diction had overtones of association, and built up suggestive tonal patterns, but the revised versions, again selecting diction and tones, employed the descriptive as symbols functioning in a total, tight pattern of symbol. This is a move on the poet's part towards the more 'oblique'. And it is to be noted that this move accompanies not only a move towards tighter poetic structure, but towards a 'deeper', a more complex and subtle meaning.

But it is death that brings thoughts and feelings that are most difficult to express, and the death of Arthur Hallam brought to Tennyson a sense of the inadequacy of language as a medium. And this sense led him to what might be termed an exploration of 'oblique' modes of expression. One of the most brilliant is *On a Mourner*, written immediately after the shocking news of Hallam's death. It is in seven five-line stanzas, and deserves detailed examination.

> Nature, so far as in her lies,
>   Imitates God, and turns her face
> To every land beneath the skies,
>   Counts nothing that she meets with base,
>   But lives and loves in every place . . .

This opening stanza is indeed oblique: its relevance has to be sought for. And the style, an abstract philosophical statement on the relationship between Nature and God, shows no open emotion. Tennyson's latest editor, Christopher Ricks, sees the theme here as 'the beautiful but ineffective consolations of Nature', yet a close reading will show that he is mistaken. In a poem on a subject so urgent to Tennyson, we can take it that he means what he says. In this stanza he is asserting a genuine analogy between Nature and God; Nature *imitates* God, 'so far as in her lies'. Within limits, then, what Nature seems to teach us is an authentic divine message. Like God, Nature turns her face to the whole world; like God, Nature 'counts nothing that she meets with base', seeing all as part of one created whole; and like God, Nature 'lives and loves' everywhere. The limitation is that Nature is a finite and physical analogy of the infinite and spiritual God, so that to say that we live and have our being in Nature is true in a physical sense, as a counterpart of the spiritual truth that it is God in whom we live and have our being. Every phrase in the stanza applies both to Nature and to God, and the stanza is as much about God as about Nature. The last line is thus a powerful affirmation of faith: Nature 'lives and loves' in a physical sense throughout the world, is indeed the principle of physical life and love, imitating as analogy, and thus giving us a physical symbol of, the spiritual life and love of the omnipresent God. In *In Memoriam* Tennyson asks the rhetorical question, 'Are God and Nature then at strife?' Too many readers fail to notice that this *is* a rhetorical question, to which Tennyson's answer is a very decisive, 'No! They cannot be!'

The second stanza is continuous syntactically with the first. In fact the first three stanzas form a single sentence, but the second is in a quite different mode:

> Fills out the homely quickset-screens,
> And makes the purple lilac ripe,
> Steps from her airy hill, and greens
> The swamp, where hummed the dropping snipe,
> With moss and braided marish-pipe . . .

The grammatical subject of the sentence is still 'Nature'; in this stanza the general and philosophical analogy of the opening is suddenly succeeded by specific concrete detail of Nature's activity, her 'living and loving'. The emphasis is on growth and life, on the renewal of life in the Spring. The diction and tonalities are deliberately rich, contrasting with the austerity of the first stanza. The analogy of God and Nature is continued in the one detail of the stanza which is not a concrete description of the physical activity of Nature: 'Steps from her airy hill'. The implication is that just as Nature, a physical power transcending the actual beings that live in Nature, in the Spring descends and gives them new life, so God, the transcendent spiritual power, renews the life of the dead. The renewal of natural life in the Spring thus becomes, thanks to the analogy, which is valid even if limited, an intimation of immortality: the dead are not finally and eternally dead. This is why Spring touches our heart with a joy and hope which are not illusory: Nature, as the third stanza goes on to say,

> . . . on thy heart a finger lays,
> Saying, 'Beat quicker, for the time
> Is pleasant, and the woods and ways
> Are pleasant, and the beech and lime
> Put forth and feel a gladder clime.'

The analogy is sustained still in the double meaning, literal and figurative, of the 'gladder clime'. Our own 'natural' sense of joy and new life with the renewal of Nature, the 'quicker' beating of our hearts ('quicker' in both senses, 'faster' and 'more alive') are not only physical responses to Nature but also intuitive recognitions of the intimations.

> And murmurs of a deeper voice,
>   Going before to some far shrine,
> Teach that sick heart the stronger choice,
>   Till all thy life one way incline
>   With one wide Will that closes thine.

This, the central fourth stanza, turning back to a more abstract and philosophical mode, contains the core of the poem's 'doctrine'. Nature's intimations of renewed life and of an order governed by principles of life and love are supported and reinforced by 'murmurs of a deeper voice', an inner voice of our own conscience whose Anglo-Saxon name, *inwit* 'inner knowledge' now recalls for us its real meaning. This voice, it will be noted, is a 'deeper voice' than Nature's; it speaks more directly than by analogy, even if it only 'murmurs'. It indicates the true way if not the exact and detailed nature of the end of the journey; it is, as the Cambridge Platonists liked to call it, the 'candle of the Lord', a limited but sufficient and valid part of the divine light. It 'goes before to some far shrine', teaching acceptance of the ways of God as benevolent, teaching, in the words of Tennyson's favourite Christian poet, that in *la sua volontate è nostra pace*, in 'His will is our peace'.

The tone of the poem now changes to the elevated tone of the formal ode, using the dignified device of personification in something like the pictorial style of Collins – the mode is essentially an eighteenth-century one.

> And when the zoning eve has died
>   Where yon dark valleys wind forlorn,
> Come Hope and Memory, spouse and bride,
>   From out the borders of the morn,
>   With that fair child betwixt them born.

Tennyson first wrote 'fringing eve', and changed it to 'zoning' before publication. Since a fringe is an edge, and a zone can also be taken to be a boundary, it seems likely that the change is partly for euphony, partly to suggest more clearly a boundary between two regions, 'fringe' being an edge to one only. The 'eve' separates day from night. When eve has died, all is night, and we are in the 'dark valleys'. The allusions to night as death, and to the 'valley of the shadow' are clear enough. But night itself has another fringe, 'the borders of the morn', whence come the wedded Hope and Memory and their child. The hope is the hope of immortality: that the night of death leads to the morning of re-birth. It is important to note that Tennyson does not make Hope the child of Memory, but the spouse. Memory, the re-membering of the dead by the mourner, does not create Hope; they come together, inseparable, accompanied by their child, presumably Love, born of and nurtured by Hope and Memory.

The last two stanzas again form a single sentence, the first of the stanzas rushing on into the second, but they contain two distinct poetic modes. The first continues the style of the fifth stanza, but pivots on the phrase it shares with the seventh stanza into a new mode:

> And when no mortal motion jars
> The blackness round the tombing sod,
> Through silence and the trembling stars
> Comes Faith from tracts no feet have trod,
> And Virtue, like a household god
>
> Promising empire; such as those
> Once heard at dead of night to greet
> Troy's wandering prince, so that he rose
> With sacrifice, while all the fleet
> Had rest by stony hills of Crete.

The diction of the first line of stanza six offers some difficulties, which the manuscript readings help to clarify. Tennyson first wrote: 'And when no human murmur jars The darkness round the tombing sod'. The 'tombing sod' is the grave, and the dark-ness (replaced by 'blackness', which emphasizes the mood of sorrow and desolation, rather than the mixed associations of darkness, which may suggest absence of intellectual illumination) is the pervasive sense of death and sorrow. 'Mortal' replaces 'human', partly as an equivalent term, but partly to emphasize the inevitability of the death of the human body: we who mourn the dead and who cry out against death are ourselves mortal. 'Jars' is the most powerful, and most unexpected, word in the passage. It is used here in the sense of 'makes jarring, or discordant'. 'Human murmurs', complaints and rebellions against death, resentment of the fact of death, make the blackness round the grave a disturbed one, filled with a sense of harmony broken and destroyed. 'Mortal motion', the published reading, is less specific than 'murmurs', and suggests not only the movement in the mind of the mourner of rebellious ideas, but all sorts of agitation of ideas, emotions and of the spirit. It is only when death and the blackness are accepted, when the 'sick heart' has learnt 'the stronger choice', when the agitated human will inclines to the 'one wide Will', when no 'mortal motion' disturbs the calm of acceptance, that Faith and Virtue will come with their assurances. They come, not through the human clamour, but 'through silence and the trembling stars', and not from the human consciousness, but 'from tracts no feet have trod'. Faith, as the catechism defines it, is 'a supernatural gift of God'.

This rather lengthy commentary on a very few lines seems necessary, not simply as exposition of their meaning, but as an examination of the poet's technique at this particular point in the poem. The diction is extremely simple, but the meaning is not. The words have a surface appearance of directness, but the expression is decidedly 'oblique', demanding a thoughtful dwelling on each word and phrase until the whole sense coheres. The passage brings the reader to a reflective and contemplative pause which in itself induces a kind of calm, 'all passion spent'. And at this moment the poet once again modulates to a quite different mode. The word Virtue has both Christian and classical connotations; as we move here from Faith to Virtue, the Christian is dominant, but the introduction of 'household god' moves us abruptly to a classical context, and 'promising empire', followed by the allusion to Aeneas, seems to abandon the Christian for the purely classical. But behind the allusion lies the long tradition that saw Virgil as something more than the great Roman epic poet, that saw him also as a poet with some prophetic foresight of Christian truths, so that his fourth eclogue was seen as a prophecy of the birth of Christ, and was known as the 'Messianic eclogue', while the theme of the *Aeneid, Italiam sequor*, became something like a classical *Pilgrim's Progress*, of man's persistence in the search for the Celestial City. The promise of empire, then, given to Aeneas by the gods, and fulfilled by them because of his steadfast virtue and piety, is seen as a parallel to the Christian promise. The scene in the *Aeneid* which Tennyson's lines recall depicts Aeneas at a moment of blackness, when his task of seeking the new land seemed most remote of fulfilment, and as he and his exhausted men lay by the 'stony hills of Crete', in the wasteland, it seemed, of their hopes. But the voices came to Aeneas, sleepless with care, confirming the promise, *venturos tollemus in astra nepotes Imperiumque urbi dabimus* 'we will lift up to the stars your sons that are to be, and give empire to their city'.

That Tennyson should end this very personal poem with its dominant theme of acceptance of the divine will, and acceptance of death as consonant with divine benevolence and providence, and its affirmation of the promise of spiritual immortality, not with comforting echoes of the New Testament, but with an allusion to the Aeneid, may at first sight seem strange. But it is again part of the general obliqueness of the whole poem. Its very unexpected-ness commands the attention of the reader, and makes him reflect on the meaning and overtones. Moreover, since the *Aeneid* may be read at more than one level, so may this allusion. It calls up, of course, the whole context of Virgil's poem, the adventures, perils, and discouragements Aeneas had to undergo, his firmness of will, his piety, his abiding sense of purpose, and the trans-cendent importance of his quest. In purely human terms, it expresses the need Tennyson himself says he felt at this time, of the 'need of going forward and braving the struggle of life', that 'still life must be fought out to the end'. He spoke these words of his poem *Ulysses*, but Aeneas is also a Ulysses-figure. This purely human meaning is reinforced, as we have seen, by the religious interpretation traditionally attached to Virgil's poem.

Here, then, is a poem of intense personal concern, written in what superficially seems a very simple but curiously remote manner. It never seems to approach the immediacy of personal bereavement and anguish directly, yet this underlies every word. The intensity of personal feeling is disciplined into a calm, the calm necessary for Faith to be heard. At least four different poetic modes, echoes of different genres, are used, each lending its own tone, its own kind of formality. And through it all runs a thread of logical development, from the intimations of Nature to the intimations of conscience, to the submission of the will to the divine Will, to the establishment of the calm in which the voice of Faith may be heard.

A simpler and even more familiar example of oblique expression of the same deep sorrow and anguish over Hallam's death is found in *Break, break, break*. Readers find this much more immediately moving than *On a Mourner*, which suggests that it is less thoroughly oblique. It does indeed include some very direct lines:

> And I would that my tongue could utter
> The thoughts that arise in me ...
> But O for the touch of a vanished hand,
> And the sound of a voice that is still! . .
> But the tender grace of a day that is dead
> Will never come back to me.

The technique is in fact a mixture of direct and oblique, and it is the interplay and cooperation of the two modes that give the poem its great power. The oblique can and does operate at a level of pure suggestion. The opening lines make a very strong impression, partly from the suggestive quality of their tonality and rhythm – the great pauses after each tolling 'Break', and the hard slow impact of the long monosyllables, 'cold gray stones, O Sea!' – and partly from the vague symbolic suggestions of the rolling waves breaking on a rocky shore. For Tennyson, the symbolism is much more precise. Its full meaning for him appears explicitly in a number of poems: in the words repeatedly applied to Arthur in *Idylls of the King*, 'From the great deep to the great deep he goes'; in many passages in *In Memoriam*, particularly in the Epilogue; and most completely in the poem on the birth of his son, Hallam, *De Profundis*. Physically, the individual being is constituted by the setting of boundaries to part of the vast flux of matter that is the physical cosmos. The actual atoms and molecules within the human body are constantly changing, the body not being identical in its constituent atom from one instant to the next, but the boundaries that define the individual shape remain until death, when all again joins the flux. In similar or analogous fashion, the human soul is 'struck out of bounds', that is, its finite identity is created by the setting of limits to part of the infinite soul: in the strict sense of the word, it is 'defined' out of the infinite or 'undefined'. As Tennyson watches the waves, he sees them as forms, shapes, defined out of the vast flux of the ocean, never for an instant made up of the same particles of water, yet retaining their shape and identity until they break on the shore and their water is sucked back, shapeless, into the sea. What he sees also, symbolically, is the endless procession of human lives to death, the shaped congregations of particles we call men, holding their forms and identities until the moment when they break on the cold gray stones of death and merge once more in the flux. But the lines of *Break, break, break* contain more than the vision of death. The Sea is capitalized, and addressed with a formal vocative, and the gray stones, which might ordinarily be thought of as opposed to the sea, and which are obviously 'the destructive element' here, are twice described as 'Thy' stones, 'Thy' crags. The sea thus becomes a symbol, not simply of life, or of the physical flux from which life emerges and with which it is remerged, but of a unified system containing both life and death, and, by the capitalization, of a principle behind both life and death. The lines thus contain an acceptance, along with their sorrow and questioning.

The second quatrain, 'O well for the fisherman's boy . . . O well for the sailor lad', is indirect in another fashion. It is well for those boys and lads who can still shout and sing, joyously alive: exclamation marks lend force also to the unstated converse: 'Ill fare those who are dead'. The third quatrain moves to another symbol, the stately ships that 'go on To their haven under the hill'. The symbol of life as a voyage, with a safe haven at its end, is a familiar one. But both quatrains are ambiguous. The second can either contrast the living and the dead, or, as in *In Memoriam*, be asking, 'Is it well also for the dead?' 'How fares it with the dead?' And the third can either be affirming a celestial haven, which nonetheless leaves the bereaved longing for the lost physical presence, or it can be asking, 'Ships come safely at last to their haven, but is there a celestial haven to which man comes at the end of his voyage? To what haven has Hallam come?' The two central quatrains, then, are not clearly affirmative, and the direct statements keep pressing the sense of immediate loss, even in the affirmation of the final stanza. It is important to note that the poet's 'tongue' can 'utter' certain of the 'thoughts' that arise in him: the direct expression of his grief is 'uttered' in plain and clear language. The rest cannot be 'uttered', that is, brought directly out of him, by his 'tongue', that is, by direct speech; they can only be outlined, as it were, by the suggestions of symbol.

It is *In Memoriam*, however, that brings most sharply to a focus the problems of the limitations of language, and illuminates most fully the nature of those problems. The first is one that Browning sees more clearly, or at least analyses more precisely, than Tennyson. In a brilliant passage in *Sordello*, Browning notes how incapable language is of capturing the immediate complex totality of experience. Language is by its nature a linear and analytic medium; it consequently has to break up the whole experience into parts, which, though simultaneous in the actual, it can only present in succession. The imaginative reader is left to try to reconstruct the simultaneous whole from these successive parts. Browning's experiments in syntax are often intended to overcome to some extent this linear kind of analysis by building language itself into a complex pattern. Some pieces of the whole experience will be fitted in parentheses within other pieces, and the whole syntactical structure kept incomplete until, as it were, all the bits are assembled, if not simultaneously, at least in a single burst of reading. Tennyson never tries this sort of stylistic solution to the problem, perhaps because he has not analysed it in Browning's fashion, but largely because it creates difficulties for the reader by sacrificing clarity for the sake of complexity. In *In Memoriam*, particularly in the first half of the poem, he emphasizes again and again the inadequacy of language to convey the full depth and complexity of the states of mind and feeling he is using it to depict.

> I sometimes hold it half a sin
>   To put in words the grief I feel;
> For words, like Nature, half reveal
> And half conceal the Soul within.
>
> But, for the unquiet heart and brain,
>   A use in measured language lies;
>   The sad mechanic exercise,
> Like dull narcotics, numbing pain.
>
> In words, like weeds, I'll wrap me o'er,
>   Like coarsest clothes against the cold:
>   But that large grief which these enfold
> Is given in outline and no more. (V)

The comparison with Nature, the physical universe which partly reveals, partly conceals the divine Spirit behind it, and the image of the coarse funeral garments which partly reveal, partly conceal the wearer, showing only a rough human outline, give a stronger impression here of concealment than of revelation. Trying to put the grief into words seems 'half a sin', clearly because of the falsification involved. The poet consequently finds the verse useful, not to the normal end of poetry – the lively presentation of true human experience – but as a mechanical therapy for the poet, a narcotic exercise for the 'unquiet heart and brain'.

It is worth noting, too, how much Tennyson conveys in this section on the inadequacy of language, by the use of very simple language and image. 'Weeds' (usually thought of as 'widow's weeds') are worn as an expression of grief and of respect and love for the dead. Tennyson is indeed wrapping himself in 'words, like weeds'; he is fashioning a verbal garment of grief and love in honour of Hallam. Again, the garment, made of coarsest cloth, protects against the cold – the cold of death and of doubt. And the garment is shaped in outline by the 'large grief' it enfolds. The images create a most vivid sense of the complex feelings, in which the grief itself needs protection, in which sorrow is at once 'cruel fellowship', 'sweet and bitter in a breath', and in which words are a public expression of love and sorrow and at the same time a protective concealment.

He speaks again, in XX, of 'the lesser griefs that may be said': his 'lighter moods are like to these',

> That out of words a comfort win;
> But there are other griefs within,
> And tears that at their fountain freeze . . .

Again, in canto LII, 'My words are only words, and moved Upon the topmost froth of thought'. And in XLVIII:

> If these brief lays, of Sorrow born,
> Were taken to be such as closed
> Grave doubts and answers here proposed,
> Then these were such as men might scorn:

> Her care is not to part and prove;
> She takes, when harsher moods remit,
> What slender shade of doubt may flit,
> And makes it vassal unto love:

And hence, indeed, she sports with words,
     But better serves a wholesome law,
     And holds it sin and shame to draw
The deepest measure from the chords:

Nor dare she trust a larger lay,
     But rather loosens from the lip
     Short swallow-flights of song, that dip
Their wings in tears, and skim away.

It will be noted that these lines very much modify the attitude of
canto V. It is still 'sin and shame' to 'draw the deepest measure
from the chords', which is less limiting than 'to put in words the
grief I feel'. But there is also now the implication that it *would* be
possible to draw the deepest measure; the sense of falsification is
no longer emphatically there. And the mere 'mechanic exercise'
has been replaced by an admission that, in a sense, 'Sorrow indeed
sports with words', but in doing so, 'serves a wholesome law'.
The verse is no longer a narcotic exercise to dull pain; Sorrow has a
'care', a purpose, to make the 'slender shade of doubt' a 'vassal unto
love'. The main theme of the poem, the doctrine of the reality and
permanence of Love, human and divine, and of the reconciling of
the facts of death, grief, fear, and doubt with the acknowledge-
ment of the supremacy of Love, is here expressed along with the
recognition of the limitations of language. The first two quatrains
make it clear, too, that the dominant mode of language in these
poems is not discursive: This is poetry, not a rational theodicy.

If we look back from canto XLVIII to canto XVI we shall get
some indication of how the poet has moved from the extreme
position of canto V. He has been speaking in canto XV of 'the
wild unrest that lives in woe', represented through his sense of
sympathy with a stormy evening, when

          The forest cracked, the waters curled,
               The cattle huddled on the lea;
               And wildly dashed on tower and tree
          The sunbeam strikes along the world . . .

The physical commotion of the elements symbolizes the commotion within him. Then, in canto XVI, he asks:

          What words are these have fallen from me?
               Can calm despair and wild unrest
               Be tenants of a single breast,
          Or sorrow such a changeling be?

> Or doth she only seem to take
> > The touch of change in calm or storm;
> > But knows no more of transient form
> In her deep self, than some dead lake
>
> That holds the shadow of a lark
> > Hung in the shadow of a heaven?
> > Or has the shock, so harshly given,
> Confused me like the unhappy bark
>
> That strikes by night a craggy shelf,
> > And staggers blindly ere she sink?
> > And stunned me from my power to think
> And all my knowledge of myself;
>
> And made me that delirious man
> > Whose fancy fuses old and new,
> > And flashes into false and true,
> And mingles all without a plan?

This is a most significant and interesting utterance. One cannot doubt the genuineness of the note of surprise and puzzlement. The 'sad mechanic exercise', the words woven as a deliberate protection, have suddenly revealed things the poet was not aware of in himself; the words he has just written have not allowed themselves to be woven as the poet chose: they have 'fallen' from him spontaneously. And in pouring out, seemingly of their own accord, they have 'stunned' him from his 'power to think' and from all his 'knowledge of himself'. His sense of himself as a unified and rational personality has been shaken. Can a 'single breast' contain these antithetical moods of 'calm despair' and 'wild unrest'? The question is a rhetorical one, since it obviously can. Does this mean the disintegration and fragmentation of his personality, a reduction to a delirious incoherence no longer able to separate the false from the true? Or are these merely changes of the surface which indicate no change at all in the 'deep self'? If the latter, then what constitutes the 'deep self', and on what is its changelessness founded? These are fundamental questions in the poem, which in its exploration of the nature and meaning of love, human and divine, must also explore the nature and meaning of the human personality – for Tennyson 'the main miracle'. What is of most importance here is the recognition that the words and verses thought of as anodyne exercise, 'dull narcotics', have now been recognized as revealing more about 'the Soul within' than the poet writing canto V suspected, and revealing things he was not consciously aware of. They can no longer be dismissed as trivial.

We find, consequently, the modified attitude towards language and the verse that we have noted in canto XLVIII. In cantos LXXIV and LXXV, for example, the poet writes of Arthur Hallam:

> So, dearest, now thy brows are cold,
>   I see thee what thou art, and know
>   Thy likeness to the wise below,
> Thy kindred with the great of old.
>
> But there is more than I can see,
>   And what I see I leave unsaid,
>   Nor speak it, knowing Death has made
> His darkness beautiful with thee.
>
> I leave thy praises unexpressed
>   In verse that brings myself relief,
>   And by the measure of my grief
> I leave thy greatness to be guessed;
>
> What practice howsoe'er expert
>   In fitting aptest words to things,
>   Or voice the richest-toned that sings,
> Hath power to give thee as thou wert?

The verse now 'brings myself relief', which is a very different thing from the 'sad mechanic exercise' to dull pain; it can still not express *directly* much in the poet's mind. Hallam's greatness can most adequately be made felt by the depth of the grief his loss brought; this grief has been expressed most powerfully in indirect modes.

In the later sections of the poem, the apparent antitheses and complexity found so shocking in canto XVI are accepted and understood. In canto LXXXVIII they are brilliantly presented in verses whose tone and manner are in powerful contrast to canto XVI, which in many senses they answer and complete:

> Wild bird, whose warble, liquid sweet,
>   Rings Eden through the budded quicks,
>   O tell me where the senses mix,
> O tell me where the passions meet,

> Whence radiate: fierce extremes employ
>   Thy spirits in the darkening leaf,
>   And in the midmost heart of grief
> Thy passion clasps a secret joy:
>
> And I – my harp would prelude woe –
>   I cannot all command the strings;
>   The glory of the sum of things
> Will flash along the chords and go.

The 'tenants of a single breast' are not now 'calm despair and wild unrest', but 'grief' and 'secret joy', 'woe' and 'the glory of the sum of things'. The complexity and apparent contradictions are now accepted as natural – as natural as the mixing of the senses in perception. Perception fuses sensations of sight, sound, smell, taste, touch, into a single perceived object; similarly various passions meet in a single complex state of mind, a whole simple object of emotional perception in which 'fierce extremes' employ 'the spirits' at the same moment. The unity of each perception suggests a unity of perceiver, a spiritual centre from which passions and senses 'radiate'. The bird's song becomes a symbol of the poet's song, and its instinctive affirmation of life, of 'secret joy', and of an unearthly beauty matches the instinctive affirmation of the 'glory of the sum of things' which flashes along the chords of his harp 'uncommanded'. The complexity of the unified human personality is still a mystery, but not a shock or surprise.

The change in the poet's mode of thought is matched by a change in the mode of expression, which is much more oblique than that of canto XVI, working almost entirely by symbol and suggestion. The complicated ambiguities of the first word, 'wild', for example, with its sense of natural, of the spontaneous, of the unrestrained, the multiple associations of the whole second line, 'rings' with its suggestion of triumphant peals of bells and religious celebration, 'Eden' with all its paradisal implications, and the symbolism of buds and the 'quicks', all create a rich and dense texture of meaning. Yet the section is not totally oblique, and its method is typical of that of most of the poem, in which direct statement as it were 'roughs out' a piece of the theme (or, as he puts it in canto V, gives it 'in outline'), and the oblique use of symbol and allusion suggests the depth and body. This technique is again admirably illustrated in the serene canto CXXIII:

There rolls the deep where grew the tree.
  O earth, what changes hast thou seen!
  There where the long street roars, hath been
The stillness of the central sea.

The hills are shadows, and they flow
  From form to form, and nothing stands;
  They melt like mist, the solid lands,
Like clouds they shape themselves and go.

But in my spirit will I dwell,
  And dream my dream, and hold it true;
  For though my lips may breathe adieu,
I cannot think the thing farewell.

The vision of the ultimate impermanence of the physical world, in which geological time, seen in relation to eternity, flickers by as in time-lapse cinematography, so that mountains rise up, are worn down by erosion, sink below seas, are elevated again, and the 'solid lands' melt and flow and change shape like clouds, affirms the permanence of spirit, the changeless. The vision of the earlier part of the poem, of ephemeral man in a permanent Nature, based (by 'lying Sorrow') on a consideration of man merely as part of Nature, is transposed or reversed to that of the immortal and permanent human spirit dwelling for a brief time in an impermanent Nature. The poet's 'lips', symbol of his natural self, may 'breathe adieu' to his dead friend, but the immortal self cannot 'think the thing farewell'. The phrase 'think the thing' is an unusual and powerful one: he cannot accept the separation as a 'thing', that is, as a reality.

One is tempted to think that sections of the poem begun only with the conscious feeling that the discipline of setting words into the formal pattern of the quatrain provided a distraction from sorrow, using ideas and themes which arose spontaneously, surprised the poet on re-reading with the depth of their meanings. This is certainly the impression given by canto XVI. If so, then we may say that sorrow taught Tennyson new modes of oblique expression. It is evident that his use of symbol in the poems associated with Hallam's death that we have examined differs from his earlier use, as in *The Lady of Shalott* or the Mariana poems, or in *The Palace of Art*. As we have seen, in those poems, as revised for 1842, the symbols are tightly organized in relation to the theme. The very different structure of *In Memoriam*, and its complexity of themes, naturally limits this sort of tight organization to single sections, or to echoes carried from one section to another. But there are a great many sections which seem deliberately to avoid a closely related texture of symbol, or a pattern of symbol with readily accessible meaning. The poet seems to mix 'public' symbols of universal if wide significance, with some that are nearer to being private ones. Canto LXX will illustrate this practice: The theme is connected with Tennyson's distinction between the inner will, the 'heart', which is the source of stubborn affirmations, which refuses to 'think the thing farewell', and conscious deliberate 'willing'. The poet, the 'I' of the poem, has been trying by conscious effort to bring back a sense of his dead friend's presence. He has prayed in canto L,

> Be near me when my light is low,
>   When the blood creeps, and the nerves prick
>   And tingle; and the heart is sick,
> And all the wheels of Being slow.

Now he records the defeat of the conscious will, but the arrival of reassurance when he ceases to strive: while faith is an affirmation of the inner will, it is also a gift; it is not to be commanded by the conscious will.

> I cannot see the features right,
>   When on the gloom I strive to paint
>   The face I know; the hues are faint
> And mix with hollow masks of night;
>
> Cloud-towers by ghostly masons wrought,
>   A gulf that ever shuts and gapes,
>   A hand that points, and pallèd shapes
> In shadowy thoroughfares of thought;
>
> And crowds that stream from yawning doors,
>   And shoals of puckered faces drive;
>   Dark bulks that tumble half alive,
> And lazy lengths on boundless shores;
>
> Till all at once beyond the will
>   I hear a wizard music roll,
>   And through a lattice on the soul
> Looks thy fair face and makes it still.

The first quatrain is very direct, the only phrase full of extra suggestion being the last one, 'hollow masks of night', where each word sets up a mass of overtones which are elaborated and expanded in the phantasmagoria of the next eight lines. The details of the expansion are a curious mixture of the sharply visualized and the vague, so that they convey very accurately the quality of nightmare, with its rapid succession of clear images dissolving into something dimly menacing, then into new clear images. There is a movement of association here: The cloud-towers suggest heavenly mansions; the gulf that ever shuts and gapes suggests death, at once the abyss shutting off the living from the dead and the gateway or opening to eternal life. The hand that points is a peculiar item here, in that it is very specific and easily visualized, but not specific in its significance. What hand or whose hand is it? And what is it pointing at? Is it a sign of a direction to be taken? Is it a hand that by pointing singles out the individual? Is it consequently a symbol of the individuality of death after the reminder of its universality in the 'gulf that ever shuts and gapes'? It can be any or all of these. It is followed by a succession of images of the hosts of men streaming through and from the 'yawning doors', driving on in their masses and shoals. Again the word 'doors' emphasizes the dual aspect of death as an exit and an entrance, while 'stream' and 'drive' bring not only a sense of the vast numbers but also of how brief man's span of physical life is, how rapidly he is rushed from birth to death. There is here something of the same suggestion as in Bede's great image of the bird flying from the darkness through the lighted hall out again into the darkness, or of Dante's 'I had not thought Death had undone so many'. The crowds stream from the doors, a hand points, the shoals of humanity drive on from the doors, their faces 'puckered'. 'Drive' is a purposive word, suggesting a goal and a direction; 'puckered' suggests baffled anxiety, and the direction of the drive cannot be seen; the 'pallèd shapes' are moving on 'thoroughfares' – which means ways of journeying through to a destination – but these are 'shadowy thoroughfares of thought', their direction and end are not discernible to human thought. The final images are not human at all; the 'dark bulks' and the 'lazy lengths' suggest the extinct prehistoric creatures, amphibian and reptile, whose fossils fascinated the geologists. Their appearance at this concluding point of the nightmare again has a sort of underlying logic. The sense of the brevity of human life, of the rush of time, brings along with it thoughts of geological time, of the vast changes earth has seen, of the ephemerality, in the long temporal perspective of eternity, of the species no less than of the individual, and raises again the question of man's significance in terms which had been explicit in canto LVI.

The symbols contain implicit affirmations in the view of death as a doorway, and of the 'drive' as purposive, but they also embody the fears and anxieties implicit in the opening quatrain: 'the face I know', the face of the dead individual person, the reassurance of his survival *as* a person, and the reassurance of what his destiny has become, these do not appear. It is as if the speaker is anxiously scanning the 'shoals of puckered faces' looking for the one face he cannot see; this is what is most nightmarish in the passage. When he cannot see the face, the dim assurances fade into the final nightmare of human meaninglessness.

But then, 'beyond the will', comes a real sense of assurance; 'a wizard music' promising harmony and 'through a lattice', which again part reveals, he sees the 'fair face', and the commotion of his soul is stilled. The symbol of the 'lattice' has here replaced the earlier symbol of the 'veil', indicating a stronger sense of certainty. A veil allows nothing to be seen clearly; a lattice gives a totally clear, but partial, view of what is behind it.

It will be noted that the whole section forms a single sentence, and that the movement of the sentence, governed by its syntax and its tonalities, closely follows the movement of the meaning, from anxiety to increasing agitation and finally to the slow, calm, strong and smooth movement of assurance, to end with the gentle halt, 'makes it still'. The perfect coordination of statement, symbol, syntax, and tonality makes this section an excellent example of Tennyson's oblique technique.

A final example can be taken from canto XCV, the climax of the whole poem. In it the poet, after reading his dead friend's letters, receives his most complete assurance in the form of something like a mystic experience, an immediate sense of his friend's presence, which brings with it also a powerful intimation of cosmic purpose and harmony. This is obviously an experience difficult to describe directly, and it is interesting to note how Tennyson deals with it.

By night we lingered on the lawn,
  For underfoot the herb was dry;
  And genial warmth; and o'er the sky
The silvery haze of summer drawn;

And calm that let the tapers burn
  Unwavering: not a cricket chirred:
  The brook alone far-off was heard,
And on the board the fluttering urn:

And bats went round in fragrant skies,
  And wheeled or lit the filmy shapes
  That haunt the dusk, with ermine capes
And woolly breasts and beaded eyes;

While now we sang old songs that pealed
  From knoll to knoll, where, couched at ease,
  The white kine glimmered, and the trees
Laid their dark arms about the field.

But when those others, one by one,
  Withdrew themselves from me and night,
  And in the house light after light
Went out, and I was all alone,

A hunger seized my heart; I read
  Of that glad year which once had been,
  In those fallen leaves which kept their green,
The noble letters of the dead:

And strangely on the silence broke
  The silent-speaking words, and strange
  Was love's dumb cry defying change
To test his worth; and strangely spoke

The faith, the vigour, bold to dwell
  On doubts that drive the coward back,
  And keen through wordy snares to track
Suggestion to her inmost cell.

So word by word, and line by line,
  The dead man touched me from the past,
  And all at once it seemed at last
The living soul was flashed on mine,

And mine in this was wound, and whirled
  About empyreal heights of thought,
  And came on that which is, and caught
The deep pulsations of the world,

Aeonian music measuring out
  The steps of Time – the shocks of Chance –
  The blows of Death. At length my trance
Was cancelled, stricken through with doubt.

Vague words! But ah, how hard to frame
  In matter-moulded forms of speech,
  Or even for intellect to reach
Through memory that which I became:

Till now the doubtful dusk revealed
  The knolls once more where, couched at ease,
  The white kine glimmered, and the trees
Laid their dark arms about the field:

And sucked from out the distant gloom
  A breeze began to tremble o'er
  The large leaves of the sycamore,
And fluctuate all the still perfume,

And gathering freshlier overhead,
  Rocked the full-foliaged elms, and swung
  The heavy-folded rose, and flung
The lilies to and fro, and said

'The dawn, the dawn,' and died away;
  And East and West, without a breath,
  Mixt their dim lights, like life and death,
To broaden into boundless day.

It is at once evident that although this long section presents as its theme an extraordinary experience, and hence one difficult or impossible to convey in ordinary terms, it seems to use a far higher proportion of direct presentation than the other poems we have been looking at in this chapter. Indeed, the quatrain, 'Vague words!' makes it clear that Tennyson has in fact been trying 'to frame in matter-moulded forms of speech' the essence of the experience.

A close examination of the whole section reveals an interesting formal structure. It opens with an air of informal narrative, 'By night we lingered on the lawn', but moves immediately into a long description of the summer evening, with only one more line of narrative, 'While now we sang old songs'. This descriptive opening brings us to the sixteenth line. The next sixteen lines narrate the experience of reading the dead man's letters, the next sixteen explain, as directly as possible, the nature of the mystic experience that follows, ending with the 'Vague words!' quatrain; the last sixteen return to the landscape, repeating the last three lines of the opening quarter, and describing the movement of dawn over the garden and its surrounding countryside. The poem is thus symmetrically organized, in four parts of four quatrains each. The first part is essentially descriptive, the second narrative, the third in a sense expository, and the last descriptive again. Each sixteen-line part, except for the third, forms a single sentence; in the third, the lines of exposition form a sentence, followed by the flat sentence of 'cancellation', and then by the 'Vague words!' quatrain, which is a comment, and which is made to lead into the final part by a colon. Nothing could demonstrate more fully the immense technical mastery Tennyson has by this time achieved than the complete ease with which the theme of each part is fitted into its 128 syllables.

At a casual reading, the opening stanzas seem merely a description of an unusually fine summer night, but the silence and the calm are more than unusual: they convey a sense of the preternatural, of a sort of expectancy, as though all Nature is hushed and waiting. And night itself, which through much of the poem has been a powerfully negative symbol of loss, of death, of absence of life and light, of terror and of ugliness, is here all beauty, richness and peace. The air is not cold, but has a 'genial warmth'; the bats, with none of the common Gothic associations of horror, fly round 'in fragrant skies'; the moths, with their 'ermine capes' and 'beaded eyes', take on an aspect of rich, strange, and formal beauty. The things of the night are, like night itself, not only harmless but comforting. The circle of the dark is no longer menacing, but protective, as the trees 'laid their dark arms about the field' where the white kine are 'couched at ease'. The unwavering flames of the tapers take on a symbolic significance: the steady clear flame of life and of the spirit burns clear and undisturbed; the table becomes an altar; the old song 'pealed', like the bells of a church sending out their message over the surrounding hills.

The effect of this symbolic setting is continued in the narrative of the second part in the repetition 'strangely', 'strange', 'strangely' of the seventh stanza, in the 'silent-speaking words', and in the reference to the letters as 'those fallen leaves which kept their green'. The sense of a moment in which time has come to a stop, or of a moment which is timeless, which pervades the opening description, is echoed in 'love's dumb cry defying change To test his worth'. The description becomes an affirmation, an insight, into the changeless, into love's worth – a vision of joyous or genial calm, safety, and peace suffused with beauty and love.

What is expected and anticipated at first is realized in the third part, as 'all at once' comes the sense of the dead friend's living presence, and the moment of vision of 'that which is', the ultimate reality – what Wordsworth, in similar experiences, called seeing 'into the heart of things'. The vision is one of an order and purpose, 'deep pulsations', a harmony – 'Aeonian music' – in which 'the steps of Time', what seem the random 'shocks of Chance', and 'the blows of Death' are part of the harmonious order; not random and purposeless, but 'measured out'. The moment of vision is only a moment, and once it is past, it itself seems unreal: it not only goes, but is 'cancelled', 'stricken through with doubt'; it seems but 'a trance'. The flatness of tone and diction of the 'cancellation' creates a sudden and tremendous drop from the elevation of the lines before.

The reader, as he moves on to the 'vague words!' complaint about the difficulty of 'framing' the experience in 'matter-moulded forms of speech', or of conveying it, as it is remembered, in intellectual or conceptual terms – when the experience itself is neither material nor conceptual – might wonder why Tennyson made the attempt, knowing the difficulty in advance. There could be two reasons. One is a matter of general technique, which we noted in regard to *Break, break, break*. Direct expression, however inadequate, will nevertheless give the reader an immediate rough outline of what the poet is trying to convey. It distorts by reducing to the sensory or conceptual, so that to write 'came on that which is' inevitably sends the reader off into intellectual and metaphysical questions about the nature of Being, which is not what the poet is talking about. But it does convey roughly that he has had, or has seemed to have, some intuition or intimation about ultimate reality. Yet an intuition or intimation is not the same thing as an intellectual thought, and this direct method cannot convey the *quality* of the experience. This perhaps suggests a second reason for the passage. As the poet recalls the sense of what it was actually like as it happened, or at the very moment when it was past, he naturally tried to explain it to himself, to reduce it to comprehensible, that is, intellectual terms. All his intellect produces as explanation is couched in the terms he has used in the poem, and the process introduces intellectual doubt, 'cancelling' the immediacy of the experience. What the colon at the end of the quatrain indicates, by insisting on the continuity of the last quarter of the canto with this 'Vague words!' quatrain, is that the conclusion offers an alternative mode of 'framing ... That which I became'. And this mode is oblique.

It takes us back to the ending of the opening description, inviting us to see the first and last quarters of the poem as a separate, unified entity, and to contemplate the significance of resemblances and contrasts in the symbolic pattern. The 'white kine' once more 'glimmer' and the trees lay their 'dark arms about the field'. The repetition gives these symbols added emphasis. The white kine, 'couched at ease', seem of special importance, perhaps because of the word 'glimmered'. This and its related word 'gleam' have a regular symbolic significance for Tennyson (as in his poem *Follow the Gleam*.) A dim whiteness gleaming in a dark background is always for him a symbol of reassurance, a faint but adequate glimmer of light in the darkness, analogous to the 'candle of the Lord' of the Cambridge Platonists. It is related to Tennyson's other favourite symbol of the veil. Earlier in *In Memoriam*, in canto LXVII, another poem of comfort and assurance, he ends with a symbolic pattern in which the white marble tablet bearing the name (symbol of the self) of his dead friend 'in the dark church' 'glimmers to the dawn'. Here the white kine in the dark field 'glimmer' in the 'doubtful dusk', in the dusk which is giving way to dawn.

Then, 'sucked from out the distant gloom' comes the breeze that brings the still landscape into life and motion. The expectant calm of the landscape is replaced by a tremendous movement and energy as the wind, ancient symbol of the spirit, moves over it, 'fluctuating all the still perfume' until all the air is filled with its sweetness, swings the rose and flings the lilies, again ancient symbols of love and purity (with other complex meanings), brings the message, 'The dawn, the dawn', and dies away. In this symbolic presentation, nothing is 'cancelled' – the wind dies away, but this does not destroy its message and meaning. The breeze was 'sucked from out the distant gloom', as the intuition of cosmic order, unity and love was drawn out from the poet's sorrow. The final symbol, again a favourite one of Tennyson's, is a powerful and obvious one to dwellers in northern latitudes, where in midsummer the last light of the sun in the sky moves from the northwest to the northeast, never quite fading out, so that sunset and dawn do indeed 'mix their dim lights . . . to broaden into boundless day'. Tennyson here makes the symbolism explicit with the phrase, 'like life and death'. This is the affirmation of his apprehension of unity, and of the promise of infinite life and illumination.

We shall have more to say about *In Memoriam* elsewhere, in the chapter on language and thought, where we will again consider some of the problems we have touched on. We shall there have occasion to deal with other aspects of the problem of language, aspects of great importance particularly in this poem, which it will be sufficient at this point to outline very briefly. One is that language is, as Tennyson puts it in canto XCV, 'matter-moulded': its roots are all tied to the physical; it starts as names of physical things or physical actions. It then moves to abstraction to provide intellectual concepts, and becomes adapted for the use of the intellect. But there is a whole range of human experience which is neither material and physical nor intellectual, and for this range language has no real vocabulary. Other problems lie in habits of usage. Language, by setting up categories like 'thought' and 'feeling', separates and opposes them, although in reality they are neither separate nor opposed. The old faculty psychology is an example of verbal categories which become distinct and antithetical. Again, words acquire contexts from systems of thought in which they are used, so that 'reason' has a totally different meaning for, say, a Cambridge Platonist and a Hobbist. If a word becomes narrowed and limited in its meaning, it will no longer be understood in its old, larger meaning; it is then difficult to find a word to convey the old meaning. These are problems of which all the Romantic poets are aware, and they devise different methods for dealing with them, none of which can actually solve the

problem unless the reader, too, is aware of them, and patient and
exact in trying to discover how the poet is using his words.

These are problems, however, which are most acute in attempts
at direct expression; oblique expression is a main way of avoiding
them. Tennyson's Tiresias, the Seer, had eyes 'keen to seek the
meanings ambushed under all they saw': so had the poet who
created him and, as we have seen, he ambushes the more elusive
meanings with symbol.

CHAPTER 6

Language and Thought

𝔊𝔊𝔊𝔊𝔊𝔊

THE comments Tennyson makes in *In Memoriam* on the limitations of 'matter-moulded' forms of speech, to which we drew attention in the last chapter, seem by implication to accept the complete adequacy of language, not only for sensory experience, which can be thought of as most directly connected to 'matter', but for abstract and conceptual thought, where language uses metaphors derived from the physical, as the etymology of such words as 'abstract', 'conceptual', 'language', 'metaphor', and 'derive' will show. He is at least distinguishing three areas of experience and considering how well each can be conveyed in language, and it is the third area, of experience which is neither physical nor intellectual, that he finds most difficult to put into words, especially directly. And the poem itself illustrates the comparative ease with which direct sensory experience, sights and sounds, the immediacy of physical objects, can be called up vividly to the reader's imagination. Up to a point, the intellectual and conceptual can also be presented with clarity and force, so that most readers come away from *In Memoriam* with a strong and relatively accurate notion of the intellectual doubts pressed on the speaker by 'the freezing reason's colder part'.

Nevertheless, as most philosophers have discovered, it is by no means easy to convey intellectual ideas accurately or adequately in words, which tend to have either too narrow or too broad a meaning for the purpose, or to have acquired too many or wrong sets of associations or implications, or to have developed too many quite distinct meanings. A major task for the careful reader of any philosopher's writings is to determine precisely, as far as he can, what meaning the philosopher is attaching to each of his terms. The same task confronts the careful reader of a poet when the poetry is concerned with intellectual thought akin to that of the philosopher. As compared with the philosopher, the poet suffers from two disadvantages. One is that he is writing for a very broadly defined body of readers or audience – virtually for Everyman. Even more important is the nature of his art, which seldom allows for the kind of systematic procedure and defining of terms open to philosophers. Wordworth's highly important definition of imagination as 'Reason in her most exalted mood' is unusual poetic practice, even in an avowedly philosophical poem. The poet cannot, without destroying the form of his art, carefully clear away all possible misinterpretations of his terms; he can only hope for a patient and careful reader who will clear them away himself.

The problem is particularly acute, since the poet is usually dealing with an area of thought which proves very troublesome to philosophers. 'There is no subject', wrote Thomas Reid, 'in which there is more occasion to use words that cannot be logically defined, than in treating of the powers and operations of the mind'. As he goes on to point out, attempts to narrow the terms by precise definition create even more confusion. Certainly at the popular level, the attempts to analyse and distinguish the 'powers and operations of the mind' have tended to reduce the bafflingly complex unity of the mind to a collection of over-simple, separate, and often opposed elements, so that 'thought' and 'feeling' come to be set off against each other, as if they could have separate existences, and as if they interfere with each other. Artificial concepts of pure objective thought and of pure subjective feeling are set up, and the psychological reality is lost sight of. Since it is the reality the poet is trying to convey, in which states of mind are states of thought and of feeling at the same time, and in which varied movements can be taking place in the same mind at different levels at the same moment, any approach to his work with a simplistic psychology is bound to lead to distortion and misinterpretation. Tennyson has suffered a good deal from this sort of approach, and from readers who bring to his terms their own definitions and sets of association, instead of searching patiently for the meanings the terms have for Tennyson.

It might be asked why he uses terms open to misapprehension, but where are unambiguous terms to be found? If we look at the terms that give rise to most of the problems in understanding *In Memoriam*, it will be easy to see why they create problems, but not easy to supply a satisfactory set of substitutes. One group of words is related to modes of cognition: 'Faith', 'reason', 'knowledge', 'wisdom'; and the verbs 'know', 'prove', 'see', 'trust'. In popular usage, faith is opposed to knowledge, and trusting is opposed to proving; knowing tends to be identified with proving. But wisdom is generally distinguished from knowledge, either by thinking of knowledge in a limited sense as mere accumulation of information, or as narrowly specialized, or else by seeing wisdom as a capacity for using knowledge, or as embodying a broad sense of the relations of many kinds of knowledge to the needs of human life. Wisdom is consequently thought of as a rare, rather than a universal quality, and 'wise' becomes an honorific term rather than one for regular operations of the human mind. 'Reason', on the other hand, is thought of at the popular level as the faculty which guides most normal behaviour unless overcome by strong emotion or passion, so that normal behaviour is 'rational', abnormal 'irrational'. In this context, 'reason' means primarily a kind of prudent common sense, a conformity to the general pattern of ordinary practical experience. Tennyson, in using the common terminology, is nevertheless rejecting nearly all of this popular usage. He goes back to fundamentals, and asks what it is indeed that man lives by: is it by reason? by knowledge? Do we in fact make our critical decisions by a careful marshalling of facts and an inner rational debate? Do we demand and receive proof of the rightness of our actions, of the value of our aims? What can we prove or demonstrate?

Any present-day reader familiar with the arguments of philosophers of science, with the views of writers like Karl Popper or the late N. R. Hanson, the debates about 'verifiability' and 'falsifiability' in science, will have no difficulty in following Tennyson's line of thought. Nor will those whose interest goes back a generation or two to the early developments of modern positivism in men like Ernst Mach, F. C. S. Schiller, and Jules Henri Poincaré. Their work, in emphasizing the large tautological element in the structure of scientific thought, and in recognizing, in Schiller's phrase, that 'all axioms are postulates', served to break down that naïve view of science as absolute and demonstrated truth, as a mental structure corresponding with physical reality, which was the dominant view throughout the eighteenth century and most of the nineteenth. In the earlier part of this century, books on the limitations of science became popular; Tennyson was aware of the limitations a century earlier. His awareness proceeds from more than one source: he is very conscious of how little, in reality, is the area with which science is concerned, of how it abstracts and isolates its problems, and of how far the sort of answer it gets is determined by the kind of question it asks. If you appeal to Nature, he points out in canto LVI, that is, if you ask a question in terms of naturalism, expecting an answer in the same terms, these are the only terms in which the answer will come. Question, as here, about values, and your only answer is in terms of process without values; in naturalist terms there is only the bringing to life, the bringing to death. The natural process will not reveal meanings outside itself. Science, concerned with the investigation of the physical, starts with the implicit postulate that, as far as it is concerned, there is only the physical; seeking explanatory structures in terms of mechanism, it postulates the sufficiency of mechanical explanation. Ultimately, as Tennyson sees, the procedure of science is not only a carefully limited abstraction; if taken as presenting the whole truth about the whole of reality it is self-destructive. For any mechanistic theory of mind destroys all the kind of validity we normally give to thought. If we accept seriously, as some have done, Feuerbach's light-hearted proposition, *Der Mensch ist was er isst*, 'Man is what he eats', then something the German has eaten explains why he thinks this theory, and not another. Or if, in another famous dictum, 'The brain secretes thought as the liver secretes bile', all thoughts being a result of physical secretions and hence physically determined, terms like 'true' or 'false', 'reasonable' or 'unreasonable', lose their meaning. In Tennyson's time, the popular mode of mechanical explanation of thought was in terms of 'animal magnetism', a term given most currency by Mesmer and his experiments in mesmerism or hypnosis. The outstretched fingers of the mesmerist, electrodes or aerials directing the 'magnetism' from him to the patient, are still part of folklore. It is to Mesmer's theory that Tennyson alludes in canto CXX:

> I think we are not wholly brain,
> Magnetic mockeries; not in vain,
> Like Paul with beasts, I fought with Death;
> Not only cunning casts in clay:
> Let Science prove we are, and then
> What matters Science unto men,
> At least to me? I would not stay . . .

There is irony here, of course, in the word 'prove', both from Tennyson's knowing that science can never prove anything of the sort, and more importantly, that a 'proof' which was itself a product of magnetic flux in the mechanical brain would bear no relation to what we call proof. A modern computer can produce proofs, but only if programmed by a mind. Again, if our thoughts are merely products of magnetic events, they are 'mockeries' in that they can have none of the kinds of validity and importance we attach to them, and Science itself, its form and structure determined, not by what we commonly understand as thought, but by a purely physical process, cannot have the sorts of meaning we attach to it. In fact, in a system of purely mechanical psychology, it is difficult to attach any meaning to 'meaning'.

Tennyson's approach to science was, as we know from the comments of contemporary scientists who knew him well, a very fully informed one; it was also, as is evident here, a very sophisticated one for his time. As the physicist Sir Oliver Lodge commented, he moved 'in the atmosphere of Science not as an alien, but as an understanding and sympathetic friend', but he had the advantage of belonging to both of those cultures Lord Snow sees as now separated, and which were perhaps even more radically separated through much of Tennyson's lifetime. Tennyson could approach science with knowledge and sympathy, but with a wider perspective from literature and philosophy, seeing the role of science constantly in a larger context. His awareness of the limitations of science proceeds also from his philosophical thought and from his brooding as philosopher and as poet on man and his nature. He approaches the whole problem in the broad terms suggested above: what does man indeed live by? It is obvious to him, as it is to everyone, that man would like to live by certain and demonstrated knowledge; it would indeed be a comfortable and reassuring state never to take a wrong step or make a wrong decision. But this is unhappily not the human situation. Yet neither is man condemned in fact to total indecision and inaction where he has not demonstrable certainty. What is demonstrable cannot be doubted, and there is indeed very little, and nothing of great importance, that cannot be doubted. In *The Two Voices*, the 'I' of the poem is assailed by an inner voice of doubt and despair, which challenges, 'Surely 'twere better not to be'. This voice argues with the 'I' on the basis of two assumptions: that inability to prove the value of the individual human life proves that it has no value, and that the 'I' ought at once to end a life with no demonstrable value. The 'I' rejects both assumptions, once it gets a chance to move to the attack in the debate. The voice has used the sceptical argument that it is impossible to know that life has value; the 'I' turns this back with the impossibility of knowing that it has not. Further, no one has ever truly longed for death *as* death; those who commit suicide do so in despair of having the fuller life they wanted and want. But the poem ends, after the argument has ended in a deadlock, with a symbolic opening of the study-window and a look to the world outside, bringing a sudden reminder of the arid and academic nature of the argument. No one decides to live or not to live, or feels or fails to feel the value of existence, by this sort of logic or by search for this sort of proof. Men do not hang themselves in obedience to the conclusion of a syllogism or a QED; and it would be a very naïve theatregoer who believed Hamlet would have killed himself if he had found fewer arguments against it.

The limited role of demonstration or 'proof' in the actual conduct of men's lives is further elaborated in *The Ancient Sage*, late in Tennyson's career:

> Thou canst not prove the Nameless, O my son,
> Nor canst thou prove the world thou movest in,
> Thou canst not prove that thou art body alone,
> Nor canst thou prove that thou art spirit alone,
> Nor canst thou prove that thou art both in one:
> Thou canst not prove thou art immortal, no
> Nor yet that thou art mortal – nay my son,
> Thou canst not prove that I, who speak with thee,
> Am not thyself in converse with thyself,
> For nothing worthy proving can be proven,
> Nor yet disproven: wherefore thou be wise,
> Cleave ever to the sunnier side of doubt,
> And cling to Faith beyond the forms of Faith!

Here the poet draws on the history of philosophy and some of its most fundamental questions: the existence of an external world, the existence of other selves, – both ruled out by the solipsist argument, which is virtually irrefutable yet almost universally rejected – the question of the unity or duality of human nature, and of the mortality or immortality of human existence, the existence of God – all, as history shows, undemonstrable in either positive or negative sense. Yet on at least some of these questions decision is essential. One can hardly go through life in a state of suspended judgement as to whether all the people one seems to be meeting and conversing with are real separate identities or merely creations of one's own mind. And in fact normal man accepts from the start the reality of other persons, and of an outside world, not because he has carefully rehearsed the arguments in favour and against, but by a species of immediate apprehension. And this immediate apprehension stubbornly resists the arguments of the solipsist, if it encounters them, with a confident incredulity and even amusement, refusing to be persuaded into scepticism. So it is with our sense of the value of life, and of the life of the individual human being, and with our sense of the value of justice, or of pity, and with our sense of the value of love, and of human relationship. We do not and cannot 'prove' these values, but they are what we live by and try to live by. The immediate apprehension or awareness is what Tennyson terms 'faith'.

'Wisdom', in Tennyson's terminology, is related to 'faith'; it is however not immediate, but developed through experience, so that it involves an awareness of the role of faith in the conduct of life, an understanding of the real springs of human behaviour, of the values that shape a life into meaning. It comes essentially from the fruitful contemplation of experience, so that in *In Memoriam* the sorrow that causes the speaker's suffering and that plagues him with painful doubts also makes him wise. 'Faith' as the stubborn inner affirmation – an affirmation not in the sense of an enunciation of a proposition, but in the sense of something which is in its nature affirmative, not negative, something like Carlyle's Everlasting Yea – proceeds from what seems to Tennyson the irreducible core of the personality. When all other defences have been stripped away by blows of misfortune, by fears, by doubts, there is still this hard and persistent something which still will not accept defeat and acquiesce in the meaninglessness of negation. For this inner core of being Tennyson uses the word 'heart', and for its mode of yea-saying, 'feel'. The reliance on its promptings, or intimations, or affirmations – none of which is a satisfactory term – he calls 'trust'. These are, to be sure, words with many associations alien and even antagonistic to Tennyson's meaning, and hence misleading to all but very careful and patient readers, but it is difficult to suggest words that could have served him better. The very attempt here to explain in other words something of the direction of the poet's intention by no means escapes itself from the problem; there is simply no satisfactory vocabulary to deal with experiences familiar to most human beings.

Two things must be understood about Tennyson's attitude towards knowledge, proof, wisdom, and faith. To recognize the limitations of knowledge and of proof is not to reject or despise them. Tennyson's life-long interest in science, in philosophy, in the ideas of many cultures of both East and West, should be evidence enough that he valued knowledge sufficiently highly to spend his life busily acquiring it and lamenting that he could not acquire more. Knowledge becomes the more useful as the exact nature of its uses, and the limitations of its role, are clearly understood. It is also essential to a proper respect for reason to know what it can do and what it cannot. The vulgar faith that science can do everything and solve every kind of problem does no service to science, and shows no ability to understand its nature. Further, it must be remembered that Tennyson, particularly in *In Memoriam*, is trying to convey the complexity of human psychology. States of thought and of feeling are not simple and mutually exclusive. It was the seventeenth and eighteenth century that debated whether the human mind could think more than one thought at a time, and that sharply separated thought and feeling. Tennyson knows that the human being can be assailed by fears which gnaw away at him even as he is rejecting them, can be nursing a remnant of hope while almost overwhelmed by despair, can be filled with joy on a day of spring and yet feel at the same time an undertone of sadness, or in great sorrow can still feel a pulse of action. As he knows, wildness and calm, sureness and doubt, faith and despair, trust and distrust, joy and sorrow, may not only succeed each other in the human mind (or soul), often rapidly, but can coexist at the same instant.

The problem Tennyson faces in conveying his thoughts is also very often due to the unfamiliarity of the ideas he is trying to convey. His critical view of science is, as we have noted, well in advance of the thought of his time. So is his understanding of the implications of a purely mechanistic theory of evolution. Many years before Darwin published his *Origin of Species*, Tennyson had recognized the crucial questions raised by looking at the natural

world of living things in terms of Malthus's theory of population –
what came to be known as the 'gladiatorial view of nature'. He
presents his views in *In Memoriam* and in *Maud*, both pre-Dar-
winian. He sees at once how totally the concept of the natural world
as dominated by the struggle for survival, 'Nature red in tooth and
claw', clashes with all our ideas of a morally and benevolently
ordered world. Our values of justice, mercy, pity, our sense of the
worth of the individual life, have in such an interpretation no
counterpart in the world of Nature. As Huxley was to phrase it
many years later, the Ethical Process is irreconcilably opposed to
the Cosmic Process. Tennyson puts the question, 'Are God and
Nature then at strife'? (canto LV) Nature seems to show no care
for the single life or even for the species, to care for nothing. If
this is indeed the Cosmic Process, man, with his sense of order,
with 'such splendid purpose in his eyes', with his faith in love and
in a divine providence based on God's love and benevolence,

> Who trusted God was love indeed
> And love Creation's final law –
> . . . Who loved, who suffered countless ills,
> Who battled for the True, the Just,

– man is the misfit, the abnormal, in a world where his ideals are
meaningless:

> . . . A monster then, a dream,
> A discord. Dragons of the prime,
> That tear each other in their slime,
> Were mellow music matched with him. (LVI.)

They, not man, are 'in harmony with Nature'. And this is the sad
conclusion to which Thomas Hardy comes, seeing more clearly
than Huxley – seeing as clearly as Tennyson – the implications of
such a dichotomized cosmos. For Hardy, man *is* the tragic misfit,
monster or aberration produced by the natural process, evolved
into a being with a conscious mind and conscious will, thinking
consequently in terms of purpose and order, in a universe governed
by blind, purposeless will, a mere striving at random. To Tennyson's question, phrased in their own terms, Huxley and Hardy
return an affirmative answer. Tennyson answers in the negative. If
human thought produces a theory of Nature which makes
nonsense of human thought, there is something wrong with the

theory. If Nature *seems* (and it must be noted that Tennyson constantly uses this word in presenting the theory) to be a random, purposeless, and totally amoral process, either the theory is based upon a partial view of Nature, or the questions inquiring man asks about Nature have been couched in the wrong terms. The universe is either an ordered system or not an ordered system; if it is not, all human ordered thought is an illusion, irrelevant to reality. Neither total order nor disorder can be 'proved'; but a choice must be made. Tennyson thus reaches to the very core of the problem raised by the mechanical theory of evolution; it is almost a generation later that Huxley, in *Evolution and Ethics*, recognizes the basic issue, and borrows Tennyson's symbols of the garden and the wild heath (in *Maud*) to expound it. The point of Tennyson's penetrating analysis was seldom grasped by his contemporaries, who continued to interpret Darwin's theory, when it appeared, as a teleological system of progress, so that Browning, for example, writes to Furnivall expressing enthusiasm for Darwin in terms that show no comprehension whatever of any difference between Darwin's theory and Lamarck's. Browning's own evolutionary theory, as given in the great speech of Paracelsus in the last act of that drama, is totally based on a divine teleology. Others down to our own time have not noticed the force of Tennyson's 'seems', and have taken it for granted that since they themselves look on Darwinian evolution as proved scientific 'fact', Tennyson must also, with his knowledge of science, have so accepted it. They consequently see him as torn between what science has 'proved' to him, and a religious reluctance to accept it. The truth is simple: Tennyson quite scientifically sees it as a scientific hypothesis, and recognizes what assumptions it is based on, what the limits of its evidence are, and what its implications. Then he rejects it, because he is convinced that there is in fact order and teleology in the cosmic system. At the same time, the kind of thoughts the mechanistic theory obtrudes, the thoughts that produced in Hardy such powerful feelings of human futility and impotence in the grip of blind forces, occurred to Tennyson very powerfully. They did not dominate him, or convince him, but they naturally disturbed him. Again we must recall a sense of the complexity of human states of mind, and the way in which opposed ideas and feelings can coexist in the same mind at the same time.

173

The area of Tennyson's thought most difficult for his readers to grasp, and most difficult for him to convey to them in his poetry, is that which presents metaphysical speculations, and particularly those speculations in which he is thinking along lines of thought more familiar in Eastern than in Western philosophy. The exact nature and degree of direct influence of Eastern philosophers on him is not easy to determine, and is a subject no one has investigated carefully. What seems most likely is that the natural bent of his own thinking led him towards the problems often central in Eastern philosophy, and towards asking the same kind of questions, and that he found in Eastern writings themes and elaborations of themes already present in varying degrees in his own thoughts.

These thoughts are most comprehensively brought together in *The Ancient Sage*, written in 1885. The title refers to the Taoist philosopher Lao Tzu, whose 'life and maxims' Tennyson had been reading, but the philosophy uttered by the Sage is Tennyson's own, and is not a rendering into verse of Taoist doctrine, although some of the philosophical ideas are Taoist. The poem thus illustrates perhaps the remark above, in that Tennyson presumably finds in the writings of Lao Tzu expressions, which may also be clarifications, of ideas he already had. One of the strong tendencies in Tennyson's thought, particularly in his later years, is towards a kind of universal ecumenical movement. The poem *Akbar's Dream*, in the last volume he wrote, is on this theme, that 'All religions are one', that is, 'the religions of all good men'. For the poet, philosophy and religion are inseparable; as his son reports, 'In *Akbar* he thought that the language of theology had to be interchanged with that of philosophy.' His approach to philosophy is consequently as ecumenical as his approach to religion.

The argument of the ancient sage starts from a set of ideas present in Tennyson's thought for at least half a century before the writing of this poem. He had long ago rejected the line of thought so popular throughout the eighteenth century in the writers of theodicies, astro-theologies, physico-theologies, 'demonstrations' of the Being and attributes of God. These 'demonstrations' were by *a priori* argument in the theodicies, proceeding from axioms about the nature of Being, or by *a posteriori* argument in the astro- and physico-theologies, arguing from the order of the solar system, or from the detailed adaptation of living things to their

way of life – in each case to 'prove' a providential order and
purpose, and hence a benevolent Creator. Tennyson found these
arguments to be no 'demonstration': he wrote in canto CXXIV
of *In Memoriam*,

> I found Him not in world or sun,
>   Or eagle's wing, or insect's eye;
>   Nor through the questions men may try,
> The petty cobwebs we have spun . . .

For him, what knowledge of God man can have must come from
looking within himself, not from external Nature. In *The Ancient
Sage* the inward search is presented more fully (and in essentially
Taoist terms, which are also Tennysonian terms):

> If thou would'st hear the Nameless, and wilt dive
> Into the Temple-cave of thine own self,
> There, brooding by the central altar, thou
> Mayst haply learn the Nameless hath a voice,
> By which thou wilt abide, if thou be wise,
> As if thou knewest, though thou canst not know;
> For knowledge is the swallow on the lake
> That sees and stirs the surface-shadow there
> But never yet hath dipt into the abysm,
> The Abysm of all Abysms, beneath, within
> The blue of sky and sea, the green of earth,
> And in the million-millionth of a grain
> Which cleft and cleft again for evermore,
> And ever vanishing, never vanishes,
> To me, my son, more mystic than myself,
> Or even than the Nameless is to me.
> And when thou sendest thy free soul through heaven,
> Nor understandest bound nor boundlessness,
> Thou seest the Nameless of the hundred names.
>   And if the Nameless should withdraw from all
> Thy frailty counts most real, all thy world
> Might vanish like thy shadow in the dark.

Like most passages in this extraordinary poem, this is extremely
complex and compact, 'Dive into', and 'brooding' metaphorically
suggest the process of introspective meditation prescribed in more
than one Eastern philosophy, and familiar to Tennyson in his own
experience, as he describes it later in the poem:

> . . . more than once when I
> Sat all alone, revolving in myself
> The word that is the symbol of myself,
> The mortal limit of the Self was loosed,
> And past into the Nameless, as a cloud
> Melts into Heaven. I touched my limbs, the limbs
> Were strange not mine – and yet no shade of doubt,
> But utter clearness, and through loss of Self
> The gain of such large life as matched with ours
> Were Sun to spark – unshadowable in words,
> Themselves but shadows of a shadow-world.

These moments of vision, so similar in nature to those Words-worth records, were also described in a conversation Tennyson had with the scientist Tyndall, who carefully recorded the conversation, and, one might note, took the experiences very seriously. The 'word that is the symbol' of himself is of course his own name, which symbolizes his own separate and unique identity as a person. This, it will be recalled, is for Tennyson the 'main-miracle', the ultimate incomprehensibility. It is so because of the poet's firm and persistent belief in an ultimate monism: all Being is part of the one infinite spirit. This again is a view common in Eastern philosophies, and also represented in the West in varying degrees by such philosophers as Spinoza, the German idealists, and F. H. Bradley. (The question of Tennyson's relationship to Western idealist philosophy is too complex to be examined here in detail: canto XLV of *In Memoriam* clearly refers to Fichte's doctrine of *Anstoss*. What is significant is the extent to which he seems to have drawn, not on Western but on Eastern sources, and on his own speculations.) Finite existences are created by the One by the setting of bounds (hence *finite*, and *defining*) to part of the infinite. In the epilogue to *In Memoriam*, Tennyson foresees the birth of his sister's child in these terms:

> A soul shall draw from out the vast
> And strike his being into bounds . . .

And in the greeting to his own son Hallam, at his birth, the poem *De Profundis*, he voices two greetings, one to the child as physical being, and one to him as spiritual being. Both beings, fused in the one life, draw 'from out the vast', '*de profundis*', 'from the great deep', to use the phrase which echoes through the *Idylls*. The physical being, made up of atoms from the vast, ever-changing flux of atoms that constitutes the material world, receives a shape, an outline, a physical definition, which it retains through all the continual changes of atoms within itself, through all the processes of bodily growth and aging, until death, when its atoms rejoin the flux. The spiritual being, the human soul, the essence of its personality as the body is only the symbol of it, proceeds from the other great deep which caused and contains the material deep:

> From that great deep, before our world begins,
> Whereon the Spirit of God moves as he will –
> . . . From that true world within the world we see,
> Whereof our world is but the bounding shore.

Here again the finite material world (it has a 'bounding shore') is thought of as created by the setting of bounds to part of the boundless – a view not unlike Newton's suggestion as to the nature of Creation.

> For in the world which is not ours, They said
> 'Let us make man' and that which should be man,
> From that one light no man can look upon,
> Drew to this shore lit by the suns and moons
> And all the shadows.

The 'shadows' are of course the forms of the material or phenomenal world. The shift to 'They' in this passage has a special significance we shall return to later. The 'miracle' or mystery of the human soul or personality lies in the paradox that it has a kind of unique separateness of identity, and of will, 'that thou art thou, With power on thine own act and on the world', although it is at the same time a temporary part of a universal unity. The distinct uniqueness and individuality of the human being, his conscious will, his powers of reflection and contemplation, his ethical and aesthetic aspirations and ideals, suggest to Tennyson a special kind of sacredness belonging to the human self, and a special kind of relation to God. This is why the Sage speaks of the central core of consciousness, to be reached by contemplation, as the 'Temple-cave of thine own self', 'the central altar', where the voice of the Nameless may be heard. The deep inner intimations by which man lives, the assurances described in *In Memoriam* as 'feelings' of the 'heart', proceeding from the very core of one's being, are here directly ascribed to the voice of the Nameless. To abide by them, and to trust them is 'wise', although their truth cannot be demonstrated, and is not knowledge.

Knowledge, seen either as *a posteriori* knowledge drawn from Nature, from our perceptions of an external world, or as *a priori* knowledge drawn by deductive reasoning from axioms, is useful for its own purposes, but limited: 'Nothing worthy proving can be proven, Nor yet disproven.' How brilliantly Tennyson's metaphor of the swallow makes his point! Knowledge drawn from phenomena, from the world of appearances, 'sees and stirs the surface-shadow'. How neatly, too, he exploits the double meaning of 'shadow', as surface reflection in a mirror, and as dark image. When knowledge tries to penetrate to the depths, it ends in dichotomies it cannot resolve. It is baffled in its attempt to think of matter by its necessity to think of it either as infinitely divisible or finitely divisible; space as bounded or as boundless is equally baffling. It may illuminate Tennyson's argument to recall here the apparent impasse a generation after his death over 'waves' and 'particles' of matter. The poet had been for many years fascinated by the unresolvable antinomies to which human thinking so often seems to arrive, and by the significance of the mental process. At first he saw in it, as this passage in *The Ancient Sage* illustrates, merely proof of the limits of human thought.

But now, in his later years, his speculations have moved beyond this simple recognition. He has come to see that the primary pattern of human thought is shaped in dichotomy, the so-called 'law of the excluded middle'. Our logic is based on the axiom that 'A' and 'not-A' are exhaustive and mutually exclusive: nothing can be both 'A' and 'not-A' at the same time; everything must be either 'A' or 'not-A'. We consequently set up all our thought in terms that are double, and hence all our conceptions of reality (and of appearances) are framed in duality, and we are unable to comprehend unity – except as a category to be set against multiplicity. We are able in some measure to understand that ultimate reality may not conform to our categories – as physicists later considered that matter perhaps need be neither wave nor particle, and tried fitting terms like 'wavicle' to it – but we cannot move out from our categories. If we say that God is One, we mean that he is not Many, and vice versa. If we say that He is personal, we mean that He is not impersonal, each term having in our thoughts a definition in human and either/or terms.

Some degree of recognition of the dilemma had been reached in Western thought by Tennyson's time. Kant's doctrine of categories, of frames into which the human mind fits its experience in the act of perception, sees some of the problem, particularly in relation to the question of time and timelessness. Tennyson has his Ancient Sage include the Kantian view in a broader context:

> ... With the Nameless is nor Day nor Hour;
> Though we, thin minds, who creep from thought to thought
> Breaks into 'Thens' and 'Whens' the Eternal Now:
> This double seeming of the single world!

It is the 'double-seeming' that constantly creates baffling antinomies incapable of intellectual resolution:

> Day and Night are children of the Sun,
> And idle gleams to thee are light to me.
> Some say, the Light was father of the Night,
> And some, the Night was father of the Light.
> No night no day! – I touch thy world again –
> No ill no good! such counter-terms, my son,
> Are border-races, holding, each its own
> By endless war ...

'Thy world', here, is the world of human dichotomies; the Sage's world is suggested in the first line.

It would be easy at this point to misinterpret the Sage's, and Tennyson's, doctrine, but it is important not to. The 'shadow-world', the world of appearances, is not reality itself, but it is not unrelated to reality, or totally in conflict with reality. It must not be mistaken for reality, nor must it be dismissed as mere deception. And the 'double seeming' *is* a seeming of the real single reality; it operates as a limited view of reality, not as a total concealment of it. We are placed in this shadow-world, with our limited powers of seeing, limited but sufficient if we use them rightly, and 'in the shadow we must work'. Our best conceptions of reality are right as far as they go, and an examination of the nature of our thinking can give us some notion of its limits, and hence some notion of its relation to reality.

The problem of expressing our limited apprehension of reality in language is one of a different order from the problems of language we touched on earlier. There the difficulty arose from the inadequacy of language to convey thoughts and emotions vividly apprehended by the poet but not easily put into sensory or discursive terms; the limitation was that of language and particularly of vocabulary. Now the problem is that of the limitation of human thought itself, the problem of expressing, not merely the inexpressible, but the inconceivable. Tennyson adopts a bold and simple expedient. In canto CXXIV of *In Memoriam*, he speaks of God in these terms:

> That which we dare invoke to bless;
> Our dearest faith; our ghastliest doubt;
> He, They, One, All; within, without;
> The power in darkness whom we guess . . .

He deliberately sets together the antinomies: the impersonal 'that which' and the personal 'He, They'; the singular 'He' and the plural 'They'; 'One' and 'All'; faith and doubt; within, without. In *De Profundis* he extends the method, to speak of

> . . . this divisible-indivisible world
> Among the numerable-innumerable
> Sun, sun, and sun, through finite-infinite space
> In finite-infinite Time – our mortal veil
> And shattered phantom of that Infinite One,
> Who made thee unconceivably Thyself
> Out of His whole World-self and all in all . . .

And he ends by apostrophizing God as

> Infinite Ideality!
> Immeasurable Reality!
> Infinite Personality!

Elsewhere in the poem, as we noted earlier, he speaks of God usually as He, but once as They.

The technique is to yoke antinomies together, as if to thrust the double seemings into an apprehension of the single reality. This yoking, particularly of terms like 'finite-infinite', may convey to the reader merely the ultimate incomprehensibility of the cosmos, but it is designed to do more. The phrase used in *The Ancient Sage*, 'the Nameless of the hundred names', reminds us of the Eastern doctrines, both Taoist and Buddhist, that the Infinite One, as Tennyson also calls him, includes the whole of reality. He thus includes, and is, all to which we give names. But we use names to define a limited and separate identity, so no name is applicable to the One, who is sole and infinite. No category is applicable to him, and all are. He is neither single nor multiple, since we use these as relative terms, yet he is both in that he comprehends in himself oneness and manifoldness. In his apostrophe, Tennyson takes terms we habitually separate or oppose: Ideality and Reality; Infinite and Immeasurable (the immeasurable is simply what cannot be measured. The infinite is what by its very nature has no bounds. We tend to think, especially in terms of science, of reality *as* the measurable); Personality, which to us implies defined and separate individuality, and Infinite. It also seems possible here that Tennyson intends an allusion to the Trinity, the Holy Spirit as Infinite Ideality, God the Father as Creator, Immeasurable Reality, and Christ as Infinite Personality. At all events, the poet is trying to convey through the use of the language of human dichotomized thought some sense of a unified and divine Reality in which all dichotomies, all discrete categories are subsumed. We are told that he could never read *De Profundis* aloud without being overcome by emotion, which suggests that the poem embodies his most deeply felt convictions.

It may be questioned whether a linguistic device of this sort can be poetically successful, and whether what success *De Profundis* achieves as a poem is not due to the more readily accessible ideas and images in it. And certainly in *The Ancient Sage* the power of the lines describing the poet's own mystical experience penetrates more deeply than the attempts at exposition, as does also the passage embodying one of Tennyson's greatest images:

> But earth's dark forehead flings athwart the heavens
> Her shadow crowned with stars – and yonder – out
> To northward – some that never set, but pass
> From sight and night to lose themselves in day.

Wide-ranging, penetrating, and profound as Tennyson's thought is, it is as a poet that he will be, and would wish to be, remembered. It has been long recognized that he brought to the English language a kind of tonal perfection achieved by no poet before him, and that the magnificent phrases he applied to two of his great predecessors and models can with justice refer also to himself. He too is a 'Lord of language', a 'mighty-mouthed inventor of harmonies'. But he is also one of the great masters of poetic structure, a daring and imaginative experimenter in the architecture of language. Arthur's city of Camelot, it will be recalled, becomes in Tennyson's *Idylls* a symbol of all that man builds, all that he creates, inspired by the vision of truth and beauty: its builders

> . . . came from out a sacred mountain-cleft
> Toward the sunrise, each with harp in hand,
> And built it to the music of their harps.

It is surely the finest symbol of what Tennyson himself built, his poetic city, splendid and varied in its architecture, a city 'built to music',

> 'And therefore built for ever.'

Index

Index

೫೫೫೫೫೫೫

Index

Index

Index